Kids explore Moonstone Bluff with views of the Cambria State Marine Conservation Area.

T0273907

HIKING WITH KIDS
SOUTHERN CALIFORNIA

45 GREAT HIKES FOR FAMILIES

Shelly Rivoli

FALCON GUIDES

ESSEX, CONNECTICUT

For Tim, Angelina, Rozzie, and Theo—the best hiking buddies and road trip companions a guidebook author could hope for. We did it!

FALCONGUIDES®

An imprint of Globe Pequot, the trade division of
The Rowman & Littlefield Publishing Group, Inc.
4501 Forbes Blvd., Ste. 200
Lanham, MD 20706
www.rowman.com

Falcon and FalconGuides are registered trademarks and Make Adventure Your Story is a trademark of The Rowman & Littlefield Publishing Group, Inc.

Distributed by NATIONAL BOOK NETWORK

Photos by Shelly Rivoli unless noted otherwise.
Maps by The Rowman & Littlefield Publishing Group, Inc.

British Library Cataloguing in Publication Information available

Library of Congress Cataloging-in-Publication Data

Names: Rivoli, Shelly, author.
Title: Hiking with kids Southern California : 45 great hikes for families / Shelly Rivoli.
Description: Essex, Connecticut: FalconGuides, 2023.
Identifiers: LCCN 2022043935 (print) | LCCN 2022043936 (ebook) | ISBN 9781493051496 (paperback) | ISBN 9781493051502 (epub)
Subjects: LCSH: Hiking—California, Southern—Guidebooks. | Hiking for children—California, Southern—Guidebooks. | Trails—California, Southern—Guidebooks. | California, Southern—Guidebooks.
Classification: LCC GV199.42.C22 S6864 2023 (print) | LCC GV199.42.C22 (ebook) | DDC 796.5109794/9—dc23/eng/20220909
LC record available at https://lccn.loc.gov/2022043935
LC ebook record available at https://lccn.loc.gov/2022043936

♾️™ The paper used in this publication meets the minimum requirements of American National Standard for Information Sciences—Permanence of Paper for Printed Library Materials, ANSI/NISO Z39.48-1992.

CONTENTS

THE HIKES

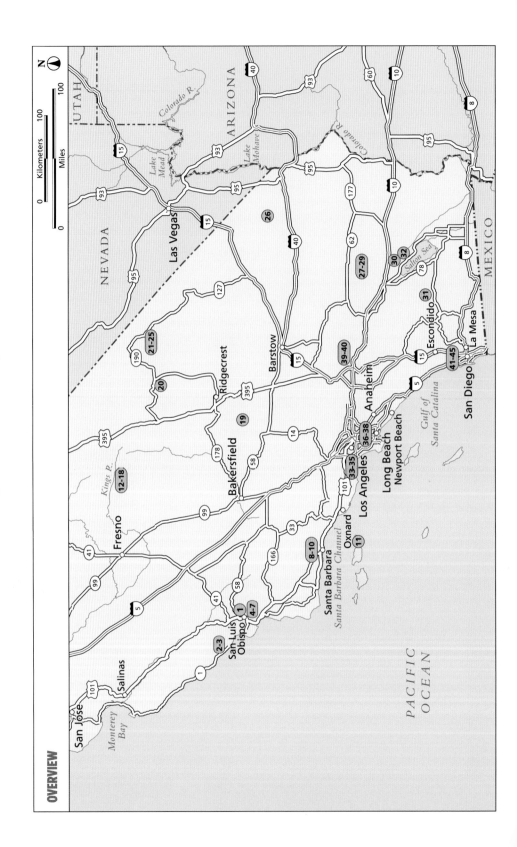

ACKNOWLEDGMENTS

I'd like to acknowledge that hikes in this guidebook take place on the traditional lands of the Chumash, Salinan, Mono (Monache), Yokuts, Tübatulabal, Paiute, Chemehuevi, Mojave, Western Shoshone, Cahuilla, Kumeyaay, Tatavium, Tonva, Kizh, and Serrano peoples past and present. I am grateful to the Indigenous communities who have stewarded these precious lands through generations dating back thousands of years, and those who continue to steward these lands today.

I also offer my deep gratitude to CAL FIRE and all the courageous firefighters who continue to risk—and sometimes sacrifice—their lives defending the California forests and wildlands we all love.

Several destination and park experts helped me in the course of this project, some going well above and beyond in support of and shared enthusiasm for this project. Special shout-outs to Lea Selig, sub-district interpreter for Kings Canyon National Park; Anna Jacobson (hiker and jogger extraordinaire) of Visit Santa Barbara; Ken McAlpine, author and communications coordinator at Ventura Visitors CVB; and Karla Kellems, director of outreach for San Bernardino Mountains Land Trust.

Thanks also to two fellow travel writers: Cheryl Crabtree, who shared generously of her SoCal contacts with me; and Jennifer Fontaine, who brought destiny to my doorstep with the unexpected invitation to author this guidebook. *Thank you*!

MEET YOUR GUIDE

In a sheltered redwood canyon on the coastline of Big Sur, Shelly Rivoli enjoyed her first camping trip as a parent with her husband and daughter of three months. She quickly learned from day hikes, camping trips, lengthy road trips, and overseas travel with her growing family, that getting out the door with children isn't easy—but exploring the wonders awaiting on its other side is everything.

Shelly's award-winning travel writing has guided families on adventures throughout her home state of California and abroad. Her family travel tips and advice have been quoted in numerous publications, including *Redbook*, *Real Simple*, *Parents*, *Fit Pregnancy*, *The Globe and Mail*, *The Boston Globe*, and the *LA Times*. She's the founder of TravelswithBaby.com and FamilyTravel411.com, where she continues to share travel advice for adventurous families. When not traveling, she hangs her hat in the Bay Area with her husband, three kids, and well-traveled standard poodle.

Shelly Rivoli with the Boole Tree, Sequoia National Forest.
ROSALYN RIVOLI.

INTRODUCTION

When I set to work outlining *Hiking with Kids Southern California*, I knew there were two possible directions I could go. The first would be what many people might expect from a title referencing Southern California—a collection of hikes in and around the major Southern California metropolises. But that, I quickly realized, would only address the southernmost third of the state—leaving out numerous incredible California hiking experiences that families should have on their radars (if not their bucket lists).

Instead, this more "geographically ambitious" book includes family-friendly hiking adventures throughout the southern *half* of California. You'll find hikes ranging from easy to strenuous (most are easy or moderate) throughout five different regions with personalities as diverse as the people who call California home: The Central Coast, Southern Sierra, California Deserts, Los Angeles and Surrounding Area, and San Diego and Surrounding Area.

I confess, there were plenty of times during our thousands of miles of road tripping that went into the creation of this book that I wondered if I'd made the right call. But there were also those moments that suddenly made it all clear that I had: listening to my kids squeal as dolphins led us out to the Channel Islands, watching them eat sandwiches on the summit of a granite dome high in the Sierras, holding my breath as we each climbed a long ladder down a dry waterfall in the Mecca Hills Wilderness.

Now, as my firstborn prepares to leave us for college, I'm especially grateful our whole family was able to share these experiences together, and that we could lay the groundwork to help lead families like yours to (and through!) some of the best hiking experiences to be had with kids in Southern California.

Happy hiking!

BEFORE YOU HIT THE TRAIL

While each individual "hike chapter" in this guide includes helpful planning tips, a map, and details specific to that trail, this section includes overall information to help you plan your family's hikes in general and get the most from this guidebook.

AN OVERVIEW OF THE HIKES

Each hike in this guidebook offers at least one of the following opportunities: excellent chances of wildlife sightings, intriguing geology, a better understanding of California's history (and prehistory), or a better appreciation of California's natural spaces. The hikes cap out at 5 miles, with most falling between 2 and 3.5 miles, with difficulty ratings from easy (some even stroller- and wheelchair-friendly, as noted) to moderate/strenuous.

Please note: Difficulty for these hikes should not be determined by distance alone. Important factors such as elevation gain, terrain, and recommended ages on foot (e.g., 3 years+ or 5 years+) are included in each hike overview to help you decide when your unique child may be ready to tackle each of these explorations.

Keep in mind, a 2-mile hike in the desert may feel longer than a 2-mile hike by the ocean. And a hike with an elevation gain of 200 feet or more (approximately 18 stories), which starts at an elevation above 6,000 feet, will not feel "easy" to the average sea-level-dwelling Californian just arriving in the mountains (pace yourselves and allow time to acclimate).

The Trail Finder section will help lead you to the Best Hikes with Kids Under 5, Best Hikes with Dogs, Best Hikes for Family Adventure, and other themed hikes in this guidebook for easy reference. Where possible, I've also included hike-specific suggestions for great places to stop and rest or enjoy a picnic lunch along the way.

WEATHER AND SEASONS

Southern California is blessed with incredible hiking opportunities every month of the year. The most important factors to keep in mind for timing your hikes are:

1. Extremely hot days can happen in any of these regions, even in the milder Mediterranean climate of the Central Coast (and even in winter months), so check the weather forecast and be sure to avoid hiking in extreme heat and get a nice early start to avoid hiking in the hottest, least shady times of day.

2. California's deserts are no place to hike in summer months—with kids or without. And many locations have serious risks of flash flooding or falling rocks during their rare rains. Each desert hike in this guide includes a recommended window of time when you're likely to experience the best conditions and trail contact information so you can confirm conditions closer to your visit.

Plan desert hikes early or late in the day for the most comfortable temperatures and best chances of shade. Shown above: Mojave National Preserve.

3. Parts of the Southern Sierra and the higher elevation mountains east of Los Angeles can get snowy and icy any time between October and April. This can lead to trail closures in some cases and road closures in others. Kings Canyon Scenic Byway (the east-most portion of State Route 180) reliably closes every winter—though when the closure or reopening occurs can change each year. For hikes October through early April, it's wise to call the trail contacts ahead of time to confirm trails (and roads) will be open during your visit.

FLORA AND FAUNA

From giant sequoias and Torrey pines to the Channel Island fox and San Bernardino flying squirrel, few places offer as spectacularly diverse—and even unique—a collection of plants and animals as hikers can find in Southern California.

When hiking with children, it's especially convenient to have quick illustrative guides to the native plants and animals in the regions you'll explore, and it can be a fun incentive to photograph and log which wildflowers and creatures you spot in your family's hiking adventures (you can even make an "animal bucket list" to check off as you go).

Wildflowers and Trees to Please

Throughout Southern California's diverse desert landscapes alone, you may hike among Joshua trees, California fan palms, ocotillo, or buckhorn cholla. And whether it's a super-bloom year or not, California's wildflowers can dazzle and delight hikers from coastal bluff to mountain summit.

Wildflowers and palms at Anza-Borrego Desert State Park.

Generally spring months are the best time to see wildflowers anywhere—and you might find them pretty much *everywhere* hikes are included in this book. As a general rule:

- Desert blooms often begin earliest in February and are generally at their peak in March and April.

- In the Southern Sierra and higher elevations outside of Los Angeles, the spring bloom starts later, often in May, and may last into August, depending on the weather.
- And while coastal wildflowers throughout Southern California are generally best in April, you're likely to find "late bloomers" of several varieties into late summer.

Yet as fun as it is to identify hummingbird sage, whiskerbrush, and mariposa lily out on the trail, it's also important for kids to learn to recognize—and steer clear of—the unpleasantries of close encounters with poison oak and cacti as well. Most trails in this guide are well maintained and should offer clear passage past these, but any hikes where extra attention may be needed for these are noted in the hike details.

California's Creatures Great and Small

From the 3-inch Townsend's big-eared bat to the 5,000-pound northern elephant seal, Southern California is home to an array of wild creatures that capture the imagination. This guidebook will lead your family on hikes with excellent opportunities to spot wildlife both on land and offshore.

A few hikes in this book are even dedicated to seeing these fascinating creatures in their native habitats and offer opportunities to learn more about the fascinating lives they lead—and some of the challenges they may face (see hikes #2 for elephant seals, #7 for monarch butterflies, and #21 for the Salt Creek pupfish). A couple of low-tide hikes are included as well that will give your family a close-up view of the impressive tidepools and tidal creatures of southern California (see hikes #6 and #45).

Of course, California is home to some creatures worthy of extra caution, as well. When hiking with kids in the habitats of black bears, rattlesnakes, or mountain lions, it's especially important to stick together on the established trail (no loose cabooses at the back of the track or rushing racers outpacing your pack).

If your dog is along for the adventure, remember that a leash of reasonable length, while generally required, may also be the key to keeping it safe in case of coyotes. And always be sure to follow any local or park guidelines concerning food storage and advice for what to do if you see these creatures during your hike.

A chuckwalla rests along the trail to Darwin Falls.

FEES AND PASSES

No permits are necessary for family-sized groups undertaking the day hikes included in this book. While many of these hikes do not require fees to park near the trailhead or enjoy the trail, others may have a day-use fee or, in the case of the national parks included, a weekly vehicle pass good for entry and re-entry up to seven days.

Each hike chapter includes information on whether it requires a day-use or other fee and which passes, if any, might be used (see pass details for more information). Since fees can change from year to year, they're noted in this guidebook by dollar signs according to this scale:

$= $1–$5
$$ = $6–$15
$$$ = $16–$25
$$$$ = $25+

Some annual, multi-park passes might save your family money as well as eliminate surprises of not having correct cash on hand, and some might even give you a chance to skip the line at some popular parks in peak seasons. The best multi-park and recreational passes for families hiking in Southern California include:

America the Beautiful Pass—For entry into all national parks and federal recreation lands requiring a visitor fee, valid for 12 months nationwide. **Note:** For your child's fourth grade year and the summer that follows, your family can get this pass free through the "Every Kid Outdoors" program. Details at https://NPS.gov.

Adventure Pass—For recreational sites in Southern California's national forests providing certain amenities (restrooms, picnic sites, and possibly interpretive signs) that require a day-use fee. Includes San Bernardino, Angeles, Los Padres, and Cleveland National Forests. **Note:** An America the Beautiful pass may be used instead at these same locations. Valid for 12 months. Details at www.fs.usda.gov/main/r5/passes-permits.

California Explorer Pass—For nearly all California State Parks requiring day-use fees throughout the state, including its popular Southern California State Beaches in the Orange, Los Angeles, and San Diego areas (which often have higher-than-average day-use fees). **Note:** The Golden Poppy Pass is less expensive but excludes most state parks in Southern California and is therefore not recommended for the purposes of this guidebook. Valid for 12 months. Details at https://store.parks.ca.gov.

California State Park Adventure Pass—For fourth graders and their families, this pass gives free entry to nineteen state parks during the school year and summer that follows fourth grade. Although most parks included are in northern California, this free pass includes Anza-Borrego Desert State Park (hike #31) and several other great parks worth visiting (and for free!). Details at www.parks.ca.gov/AdventurePass.

TEACHING KIDS TO EMBRACE "LEAVE NO TRACE"

As the saying goes, "Take only photos, leave only footprints." In a region enjoyed by as many local, out-of-state, and international visitors as Southern California, this couldn't be more critical when it comes to protecting our outdoor spaces. Just ask your child what would happen if each of the roughly 1 million people who visit Sequoia National Park in a year took home just one pinecone as a souvenir?

A young hiker adds to her digital wildflower collection at Charmlee Wilderness Park.

Thanks to our cellphones and digital cameras, it's never been easier to "collect" the specimens that most excite us out on the trail. Whether it's rose quartz sparkling in a desert wash or the shell of a keyhole limpet in a tidepool, taking photos enables us to bring these treasures home with us without even touching them.

And once home, this digital treasure trove can be a great way for kids to further identify and learn about the wildflowers, animals and insects, shells or geological formations they've seen in their adventures. It also makes it easy for them to share their discoveries with friends and relatives (and teachers assigning projects!), whether printed for a scrapbook they can compile of My Adventures in Nature or arranged in a slideshow.

In addition to leaving natural objects where they are for others to enjoy (including future generations), here are the seven Leave No Trace Principles that all day hikers and camping enthusiasts—young and old—should embrace when venturing into our precious outdoor spaces.

1. **Plan ahead and prepare.** Know the type of terrain and possible weather conditions you might encounter. Minimize impacts by keeping groups small and avoiding high-use times for the trail. Walking single file and avoiding shortcuts will limit damage to the trail and surrounding ecosystems.

2. **Travel and camp on durable surfaces.** Focus activity on resilient ground. Surfaces consisting of sand, gravel, rock, snow, or dry grass are durable and can withstand heavy use. Walk through mud/puddles to avoid widening the trail.

3. **Dispose of waste properly.** Pack it in, pack it out! This includes not only food wrappers, but also biodegradable waste such as banana peels, etc. Also practice "negative trace" by picking up trash left by others. Dispose of human waste in catholes dug 6–8 inches deep in soil at least 200 feet from any water source. Pack out all toilet paper and hygiene products.

4. **Leave what you find.** You can look, but please don't take. Leave everything that you find in the wilderness where it belongs. Avoid moving rocks, picking plants, and disturbing cultural or historic artifacts.

5. **Minimize campfire impacts.** Keep your campfire small—or go without. Use previously constructed fire rings or mounds. Only burn small diameter wood found on the ground. Do not damage live or fallen trees. Be aware of the level of fire danger of the area. Make sure your campfire is completely smothered before you leave camp. Small camping stoves are much more efficient for cooking and leave no impact on the site.

6. **Respect wildlife.** Let the wild be wild. Keep your distance and do not attract or approach animals. Never feed them food intended for humans as this disrupts their natural foraging habits. Control pets in natural areas and always keep them restrained.

7. **Be considerate of other visitors.** Show respect for other trail users. Keep voices/noises from getting intrusively loud. Obey any posted trail rules including rights of way. Orient rest spots and campsites away from the trail.

For more information on Leave No Trace principles, visit www.LeaveNoTrace.org.

THE ART OF HIKING WITH KIDS

There is a tremendous difference between hiking with babies and hiking with kids. With babies, you can pretty much strap them to you and go wherever you please. As long as they're sufficiently sheltered from the elements, nourished and hydrated, and re-diapered when necessary, babies are simply happy to be with you—especially when they sense your own happiness and pleasure in the hike at hand.

By two or three years, however, these once-portable travel companions need to be on their own two feet much—if not all—of the time. Yet they still lack certain self-preservation instincts we can take for granted with older children, like staying away from brush that's riddled with poison oak and not putting everything that looks like a berry into one's mouth.

Their reactions and reflexes around wildlife and mountain bikes are also not nearly that of their protective parent counterparts. And not every trail labeled "kid friendly" by others may feel so with these young hikers. Fortunately, the age recommendations for hikes in this guide will lead you to more suitable hikes.

By three and four years, kids will also interject a new facet into your hiking trips: their own opinions. And no matter how many times you *tell* them in advance, they may still be unable to visualize the trip you have in mind—or how fun it will be—or understand how you've already thought through the picnic lunch and snacks and binoculars that will make it all the more fun. At this tender age, they will need to become planning partners on some level to ensure truly enjoyable family hikes.

As parents, it's all too easy to take over the burden and responsibility of planning everything ourselves, but in planning for every possible detail we tend to miss one extremely important detail—letting our kids feel a part of the process! Allowing young children to help plan the snacks and think through aloud with you "What will we need if it's very sunny?" and "What will we need if it's very windy and cold?" can go a long way in helping them visualize—and feel confidence in—the upcoming adventure.

Here are a few other easy ways to help young hikers get in on the game:

- Show your child the trail map in this guide ahead of time, and show them whether you'll walk in a big loop or a "lollipop" or hike out to a point and back.

- Where appropriate, point to the overlook on the map (as an example) and explain, "Here is where we'll stop to eat our picnic—what kind of sandwiches shall we bring to eat when we get there?"

- Show them photos of the yellow-bellied marmot or flowering brittlebush you hope to see, and let them delight in the moment when they first spot it out on the trail for themselves.

The author with son Theo on his first trip to Sequoia National Park. TIM RIVOLI.

By 9 or 10 years old, it's a good idea for kids to start wearing their own lightweight daypacks when the family heads out on a hike and begin charging them with always carrying their own water, snacks, and a few essentials (including a safety whistle and small flashlight).

Little by little, they'll start to know what else they want and *should* have with them when they head out on adventures in nature, which is a wonderful thing. Because by the time they're teenagers, guess what? They'll be gearing up to hit the trail without you. And as with so many things in life, you'll want them as prepared as possible.

TRAIL FINDER

Enjoy easy hiking with very young children and peaceful views over Morro Bay on the El Moro Elfin Forest Trail.

Get started! Best Hikes for Kids Under 5
2 Elephant Seal Vista Trail
3 Moonstone Beach Boardwalk
5 El Moro Elfin Forest
7 Pismo Boardwalk, Butterflies, and Beach
10 Douglas Family Preserve Bluff Trail
14 General Grant Loop
21 Salt Creek
29 Cholla Cactus Garden Nature Trail
40 Big Bear Lake Woodland Trail
42 Guy Fleming Trail
43 Los Peñasquitos Creek Waterfall

Best Hikes for Family Adventure
11 Cavern Point Loop to Potato Harbor
22 Golden Canyon to Red Cathedral
26 Rings Loop

Whiskerbrush in bloom on Little Baldy Trail.

MAP LEGEND

Symbol	Description	Symbol	Description
═5═	Interstate Highway	‖‖‖	Boardwalk/Stairs
═101═	US Highway	⌣⌣	Bridge
═41═	State Highway	■	Building/Point of Interest
═812═	County/Forest Road	▲	Campground
═══	Local Road	⌒	Cave
= = = =	Unpaved Road	○	City/Town
┿━┿━┿━┿	Railroad	×	Elevation
— - — - - —	State Border	●—●	Gate
▪▪▪▪▪▪▪▪	Featured Trail	▲	Mountain/Peak
- - - - - -	Trail	🏢	Park Office
∿∿	Small River/Creek	P	Parking
∼ - ∼ - ∼	Intermittent Stream	🎪	Picnic Area
◯	Body of Water	🍴	Restaurant
≒≒≒	Marsh/Swamp	🚻	Restrooms
⋟	Waterfall	🔭	Scenic View/Overlook
▭	National/State Forest	①	Trailhead
▭	State/County Park	❓	Visitor/Information Center
⬚	Preserve		

Looking up the coast from the Montaña de Oro Bluff Trail.

CENTRAL COAST

With its favorable Mediterranean climate, California's Central Coast boasts year-round hiking opportunities from San Simeon down to Channel Islands National Park.

Along its 100 miles of Pacific coastline, you'll find the widely varied landscapes of weathered coastal bluffs, wetlands and lagoons, sand dunes, and ancient layered seabeds lifted by the clash of Pacific and North American plates.

Inland along the Central Coast, you'll also find wide-ranging backdrops for family hikes. Explore shady riparian corridors and sheltered oak woodlands. And hike over the rolling hills of San Luis Obispo County and up the rugged mountains of Los Padres National Forest to rewarding ocean views.

For wildlife enthusiasts the Central Coast offers prime viewing and photography opportunities. With stops on both the official Whale Trail and the Pacific Flyway, and one of the most populous monarch groves and elephant seal rookeries in North America, you'll want to be sure to have binoculars on hand and keep your camera at the ready.

This section includes eleven family hikes ranging from easy to moderate/strenuous that will guide your family through some of the Central Coast's most scenic and memorable locations.

Start with the shady
Oak Woodland Trail with
creekside sycamores.

1 THREE BRIDGES OAK PRESERVE

Hike through four of California's distinct habitat zones in a single morning, and enjoy a panoramic vista at the top of the trail. As you traverse through prime examples of sycamore riparian woodland, blue oak woodland, mixed chaparral, and coast live oak woodland, you're likely to spot wildflowers and wildlife along the way as well.

Start: At the gate beside the informational kiosk at the south end of the parking area
Elevation gain: 673 feet when hiked in full (see options)
Distance: 3.8-mile, 2-stem lollipop with shorter options
Difficulty: Moderate
Hiking time: About 2 hours 15 minutes
Ages on foot: 4 years+
Seasons/schedule: Open seasonally, typically Apr through Dec when Atascadero Creek is low enough for crossing, though earlier in dry years (check website for status updates)
Fees: Free
Trail contact: Atascadero Land Preservation Society, PO Box 940, Atascadero 93423, info@supportalps .org, www.supportalps.org
Trail surface: Dirt and some rock
Land status: Nature preserve
Nearest town: Atascadero
Dogs: Yes, on leash
Toilets: None; try public restrooms at Atascadero Lake Park less than 10 minutes away
Maps: See website and/or take a photo of the map at the trailhead—note that the Atascadero Land Preserve's map is presented "upside down" with reverse north/south orientation.
Other trail users: Equestrians and mountain bikers on lower trails

FINDING THE TRAILHEAD

From Atascadero, take CA 41 / Morro Road south to San Gabriel Road (approx. 1.6 miles south of US 101). Turn right (northwest) onto San Gabriel Road and drive 0.5 mile to Monita Road. Turn left (southwest) onto Monita Road, then right in only 0.2 mile onto Sierra Vista Road and left onto Andrita Road in only 0.2 mile more. Then go with the flow of the winding main road as it changes names along the way from Casanova to Carmelita Avenues. Small brown signs along the way keep you on track toward Three Bridges Oak Preserve.

Approximately 0.7 mile along Carmelita Avenue, you will see entrance signs to the parking area for Three Bridges Oak Preserve. Look for the sign on the south end of the parking lot concerning keeping dogs on leash, where a short trail leads to an information kiosk about the preserve and where the trail officially begins. **GPS:** N35 27.11' / W120 41.72'

THE HIKE

Adventure beckons as you approach Atascadero Creek and cross beneath Morro Road (CA 41), then cross the creek itself on large rocks laid out like the stepping-stones of giants. Watch for coast range newts along the way, which are often seen in this area. Then pause a moment at the sign you'll come upon for poison oak. The photograph of poison oak sits in front of the plant itself, giving your family a chance to see how it currently presents in the area from a safe distance. (There will be many plant identification signs to come on the hike, but when hiking with children, this one might just prove the most helpful!)

Keep an eye out for the coast range newt as you cross Atascadero Creek.

After 0.24 mile, arrive at the Lower Junction trail marker where the trail splits in two directions, making up each side (the east and west) of the Oak Woodland Trail. Head left (east) and begin your gentle ascent into the peaceful lair of the blue oak—a rare tree native only to California. Take a look at the leaves of these graceful trees, which are shed each winter and return in spring. Unlike the dark, waxy evergreen leaves of the coastal live oak, the blue oak's leaves are light, bluish gray in color. See if you're lucky enough to spot its distinctive, dark and dusky acorns as you pass—but be sure to leave them where they lie, since local deer and birds depend on them, not to mention future generations of blue oak trees.

As you approach the Upper Junction, where you'll turn left from the Oak Woodland Trail (south) onto the Lookout Trail, watch as the majestic oak canopy disappears, leaving shrubby chaparral and scrub oaks in its place. The view also opens up along this stretch revealing miles and miles of beautiful rolling foothills and some of Atascadero's historic landmarks. As you continue your climb, be sure to watch for the rock cairns stacked along the trail—and possibly lizards sunning themselves (or guarding the rocks?) atop them. Don't forget to add your own rock!

When you reach the wooden pass-through gate, where bicyclists and equestrians must tie up, lock up, or turn back, you will proceed onto the final stretch for hikers only: the Madrone Trail. In spring and early summer, wildflowers may especially flourish here, and the madrone grove may be abuzz with some very busy bees.

Sprawling valley oaks with lacy lichen shade the Meadow Trail.

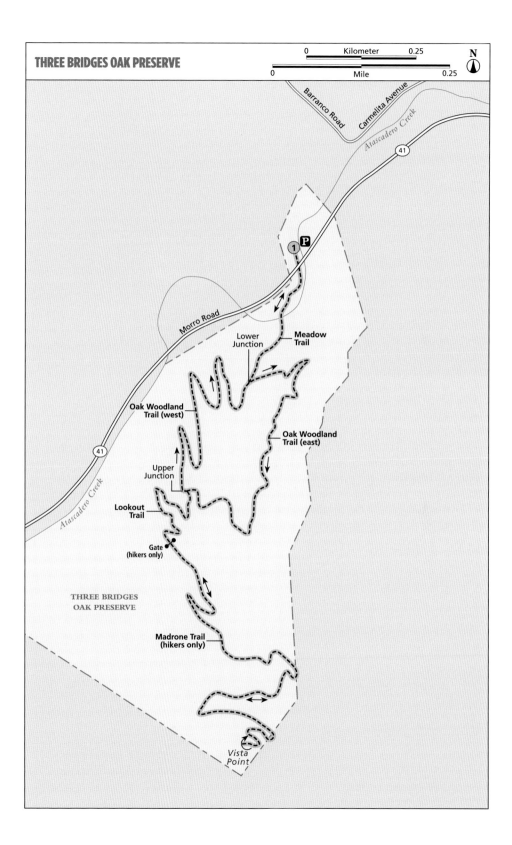

THREE BRIDGES OAK PRESERVE

0   Kilometer   0.25
0   Mile   0.25

N

Barranco Road
Carmelita Avenue
Atascadero Creek
41

P
1

Morro Road

Lower
Junction

Meadow
Trail

Oak Woodland
Trail (west)

Oak Woodland
Trail (east)

Upper
Junction

Lookout
Trail

Gate
(hikers only)

41

Atascadero Creek

THREE BRIDGES
OAK PRESERVE

Madrone Trail
(hikers only)

Vista
Point

Enjoy a spectacular view (and a snack) at the top of the Madrone Trail—you've earned it!

Gradually, coastal live oak will close in with its dense canopies of dark leaves, offering shady reprieve as you finish the final stretch to the panoramic vista point at the top of the trail. Take a look at the interpretive sign calling out all the landmarks in the distance before you, then take your place on one of the large boulders beside the oaks here and enjoy a well-deserved snack break.

When you're ready, enjoy your easy downhill return by way of the west side of the Oak Woodland Trail (you'll be turning left at the trail marker), and check one last time for newts as you traverse the Meadow Trail back toward your car.

MILES AND DIRECTIONS

0.0	Start at the trailhead for Meadow Trail.
0.2	Turn left (east) at the Lower Junction trail marker for Oak Woodland Trail (left/east).
0.8	Arrive at Upper Junction; turn left (south) onto Lookout Trail.
1.0	Pass through a wooden gate to continue on the hikers-only Madrone Trail.
1.9	Arrive at vista point; when ready, backtrack to Upper Junction.
3.0	Turn left at Upper Junction (this time north) for the west side of Oak Woodland Trail.
3.6	Proceed straight onto Meadow Trail.
3.8	Arrive back at the trailhead.

Options: For shorter options with less elevation gain, try the 0.5-mile, easy out-and-back Meadow Trail for the littlest legs, or hike a 1.6-mile easy/moderate lollipop following the Oak Woodland Trail.

2 ELEPHANT SEAL VISTA TRAIL

This stroller-friendly and wheelchair-accessible trail provides safe views of the world's second-largest seal, the northern elephant seal. Educational displays along the route help hikers understand and appreciate these fascinating creatures and the extraordinary lives they lead.

Start: At the signed trailhead at the southwest end of the Seal Point parking area
Elevation gain: 30 feet
Distance: 1-mile out-and-back with option to extend
Difficulty: Easy
Hiking time: About 30 minutes
Ages on foot: 2 years+
Seasons/schedule: Elephant seals can be seen on these beaches year-round, though peak population months are Jan, Apr, and Oct.
Fees: Free
Trail contact: Hearst San Simeon State Park and State Historical Monument, 750 Hearst Castle Rd., San Simeon 93452, (805) 927-2010; Friends of the Elephant Seals, https://elephantseal.org
Trail surface: Paved, packed dirt/gravel, and boardwalk
Land status: State park
Nearest town: San Simeon
Dogs: Yes, on leash on this trail only; dogs not allowed on adjacent trails or beaches in this area
Toilets: None; try restrooms 4.3 miles south at William Randolph Hearst Memorial Beach (possible day-use fee)
Maps: No map needed on this trail (see this chapter's map for an overview)

FINDING THE TRAILHEAD

The trail can be accessed from two different parking areas, but to do the complete trail without overlapping, start from the northernmost Seal Point parking area (also the better bet to find parking on busy days). The Seal Point parking area is 10 miles south of Ragged Point and 5 miles north of San Simeon on CA 1. Walk to the elephant seal viewing area at the southwest edge of the parking area, and continue south to where the signed trailhead marks the official beginning of the trail.
GPS: N35 39.86' / W121 15.72'

THE HIKE

Start at the signed trailhead toward the south end of the Seal Point parking area, and follow the trail southward at your leisure, taking in the educational displays and views of the seals along the easy-to-follow, 0.5-mile route. Although northern elephant seals typically spend 8–10 months at sea—making two round-trip journeys of up to 3,000 miles each year, your odds of seeing some here at the Piedras Blancas Rookery are excellent any time of year. But it hasn't always been that way.

Like many marine mammals, the northern elephant seal was hunted nearly to extinction, primarily for its blubber that was used to create lamp oil. The massive males, which can weigh up to 5,000 pounds and grow to 16 feet in length, became a popular target as whales became more difficult to find—so popular that, by 1884, the northern elephant seal was declared extinct.

However, in 1892 a last living colony of northern elephant seals was found on an island off Baja California, with fewer than one hundred remaining seals. Fortunately, the

Adult female and juvenile elephant seals seen in the spring at Piedras Blancas Rookery.

demand for lamp oil was dwindling and appreciation of our rare and endangered species was growing. In the 1920s, Mexico and the United States each granted elephant seals protected status, and the tide began to turn for the world's second-largest seal.

As their numbers increased, so too did their number of colonies, with the first California colony observed at Año Nuevo Island in 1955. In 1992 one hundred years after that last colony was discovered in Mexico (and the same year the Monterey Bay National

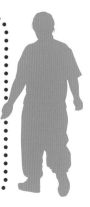

WHOAH, BABY!

Northern elephant seal pups already weigh 70 pounds at birth—and put on an average of 10 pounds a day in their first month! The best time to see pups on the beach is January through March. After that, they're already off exploring the coastal waters by themselves. You'll find more fun facts about the seals of the Piedras Blancas Rookery in the "Kids Zone" on the Friends of the Elephant Seal website. There's also a live web cam where you can see what's happening on the beaches in real time. Visit them online at https://elephantseal .org.

Marine Sanctuary was created to protect these waters), the newly forming Piedras Blancas elephant seal colony welcomed its first elephant seal pup to the family.

Today, this 8-mile stretch running north and south of Piedras Blancas Light Station sees some 25,000 northern elephant seals come and go from its shores each year. The beaches are most heavily populated during the first 6 months of the year, but you're likely to see elephant seals here in every season.

When you reach the second parking area to the south, continue southward along the viewing platform and pick up the extension trail, which continues another 0.2 mile above the rookery. When you reach the end, double back on the same course to where you began.

If you'd like to extend your journey, you can explore the informal bluff trails that begin at the signed trailhead at the north end of the Seal Point parking area (aka the Boucher Trail). Be aware that dogs are not allowed on these other protected trails.

Elephant seals rest side by side to conserve energy and help stay warm during their annual molting.

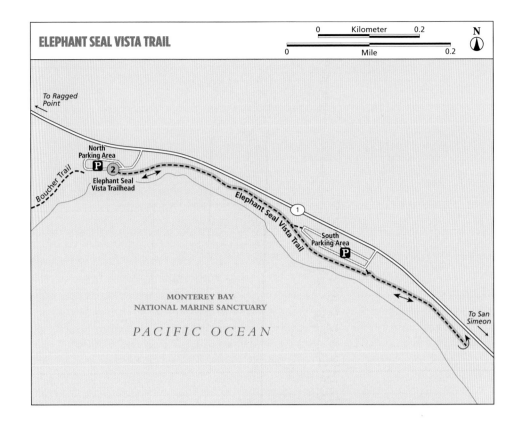

ELEPHANT SEAL VISTA TRAIL

MILES AND DIRECTIONS

0.0 Start at the trailhead.

0.2 Continue south along the viewing overlook beside the second or South parking area.

0.3 Continue south onto the trail extension.

0.5 Reach the end of the trail and double back.

1.0 Arrive back at the trailhead.

Snoozing elephant seals relax on the shores of the Monterey Bay National Marine Sanctuary.

3 MOONSTONE BEACH BOARDWALK

Start at the seaside village of Cambria for this sweet little bluff-top, boardwalk stroll providing pleasant views over Moonstone Beach, with multiple beach access points. Keep watch over the thriving waters of the Cambria State Marine Conservation Area as you go— this bluff is one of the top whale-watching lookouts on the California coast and part of the official Whale Trail.

Start: Leffingwell Boat Launch area (south of Leffingwell Creek)
Elevation gain: 29 feet
Distance: 2-mile out-and-back (with optional extra 0.5 mile)
Difficulty: Easy, also stroller- and wheelchair-accessible
Hiking time: About 50 minutes
Ages on foot: 2 years+
Seasons/schedule: Year-round
Fees: Free
Trail contact: Hearst San Simeon State Park and State Historical Monument, 750 Hearst Castle Rd., San Simeon 93452, (805) 927-2010, www.parks.ca.gov/?page_id=590
Trail surface: Wooden boardwalk
Land status: State park
Nearest town: Cambria
Dogs: Yes, on leash on boardwalk trail, but not allowed on beach
Toilets: At the Santa Rosa Creek day-use area midway along the trail
Maps: Included with brochure for Hearst San Simeon State Park and State Historical Monument at www.parks.ca.gov/pages/591/files/HearstSanSimeonFinalWeb2015.pdf
Gear suggestions: Bring binoculars!

FINDING THE TRAILHEAD

On CA 1, drive 6 miles south from San Simeon or 24 miles north from Morro Bay, then turn west (toward the ocean) at Moonstone Beach Drive. At 0.4 mile you'll see the sign for Leffingwell Landing Boat Launch on your right (ocean-side). Use this small free parking area or available free street parking here along Moonstone Beach Drive. You'll see the unmarked boardwalk trail begin at the north end of the Leffingwell Landing Boat Launch parking area. **GPS:** N35 34.84' / W121 07.09'

THE HIKE

Start at the unassuming trailhead where the boardwalk begins by the Leffingwell Landing Boat Launch, and continue south with views of the beach and ocean to your right (west) and Cambria's "front row" inns and restaurants to your left (east) across Moonstone Drive.

You'll see occasional short trails with steps leading from the boardwalk down to the beach, which you can alternatively walk on for stretches of this hike if you prefer; just remember no dogs are allowed on this beach. (Beachcombing for "moonstones" on the return trip can be an especially fun way to close out this hike.)

Following the boardwalk path, you'll come upon viewing decks at 0.4 mile and again at 0.7 mile, where it could be well worth pausing and taking a look with binoculars. The waters directly off Moonstone Beach are part of the Cambria State Marine Conservation Area, which is also part of the greater Monterey Bay National Marine Sanctuary. What's more, this location is a designated Whale Trail site, considered to be one of the best places

Above left: The Moonstone Beach Boardwalk Trail is all about easy hiking with incredible coastal views.
Above right: As this windswept cypress can attest, it can get a little windy on the Moonstone Beach Boardwalk Trail. Bring a good jacket and snug hats in case.
Below: Have a seat on one of the benches along the way and watch for wildlife in the water at this official Whale Trail site.

THE START OF SOMETHING—HUGE?

At birth, the average humpback whale already weighs 1 ton and can be up to 16 feet long—that's more than one story tall! Adult female humpbacks are generally larger than males and can weigh up to 40 tons and measure up to 50 feet long. Yet they're the most active of whales when it comes to above-the-water acrobatics. As you hike near the ocean, keep your eye out for one splashing its long, pectoral fins. If you're lucky, you may even see one breach out of the water.

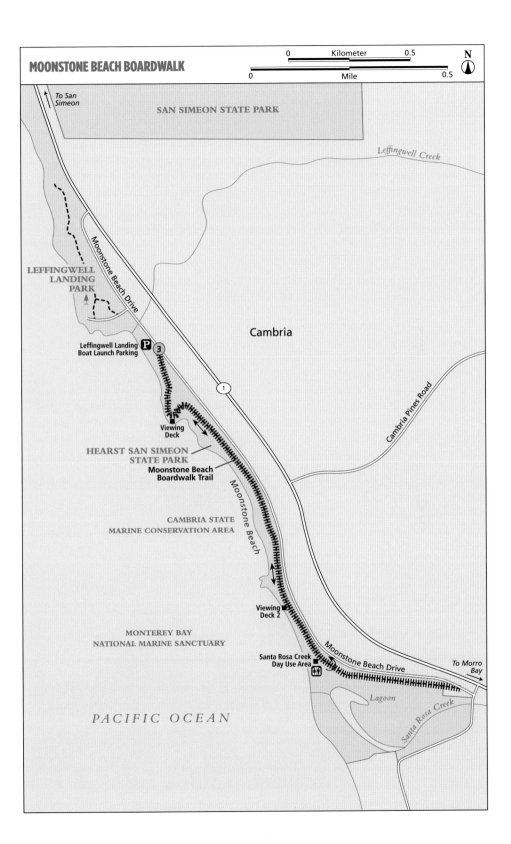

MOONSTONE BEACH BOARDWALK

0 | Kilometer | 0.5
0 | Mile | 0.5

N

To San Simeon

SAN SIMEON STATE PARK

Leffingwell Creek

Moonstone Beach Drive

LEFFINGWELL
LANDING
PARK

Cambria

Leffingwell Landing
Boat Launch Parking **P** ③

Viewing
Deck

HEARST SAN SIMEON
STATE PARK

**Moonstone Beach
Boardwalk Trail**

Moonstone Beach

CAMBRIA STATE
MARINE CONSERVATION AREA

Cambria Pines Road

MONTEREY BAY
NATIONAL MARINE SANCTUARY

Viewing
Deck 2

Santa Rosa Creek
Day Use Area

Moonstone Beach Drive

*To Morro
Bay*

Lagoon

Santa Rosa Creek

PACIFIC OCEAN

to view marine mammals from land between southern California and northern British Columbia.

While there's wildlife to be spotted any time of year, there's added excitement as both humpback and gray whales cruise along here during their annual migrations. Here's a quick overview of what your family might see and when:

- **Gray whales** can be seen here traveling south for the winter starting in October and swimming north starting in mid-February when the mothers and calves are easiest to spot as they travel closer along the shore. Watch for their signature heart-shaped "blow" above the water (the wet air exhaled through the blowhole).

- **Humpback whales** are most commonly seen here in spring and summer months, but especially in summer when large numbers congregate around the Monterey Bay area to feast on the abundant schools of small fish. If you're lucky, you'll see them perform some of the aquatic gymnastics they're known for.

- **Pacific white-sided dolphins**, **sea otters**, **harbor seals**, and **California sea lions** make regular appearances here year-round.

As you continue south, past the second viewing deck, you'll gain some distance from the village as the bluff widens. The wooden boardwalk inserts photogenic curves through the coastal scrub and ice plant. Occasional benches face the ocean, inviting you to rest or snack with a view.

At the 1-mile mark, you'll arrive at the Santa Rosa Creek day-use area entrance, with the restrooms conveniently close to the trail (continue on the boardwalk trail until you see the access path down to the restrooms on your right). You can double back from here or continue on for as much of the remaining 0.5 mile of the trail as you care to explore as it turns inland and passes by an estuary (then gets less interesting beyond).

On your return, you might opt to take any of the pathways down to Moonstone Beach, where beachcombers will delight in hunting for the beach's namesake rocks. Although they aren't true "moonstones," these tumbled agates are still fun to find among the seashells, driftwood, and seaweed that populate this beach. While you're at it, you might also find bits of jade, jasper, or sea glass. And if you've timed your visit with low tide, you can also explore the tidepools at the north end of this beach before returning up to the boardwalk and trailhead where you began.

MILES AND DIRECTIONS

- **0.0** Start at the trailhead.
- **0.4** Reach Moonstone Beach Boardwalk Deck.
- **0.7** Arrive at Seal View Beach Deck.
- **1.0** Come to Santa Rosa Creek day-use parking area with restrooms. Reverse course back to the trailhead. (**Option:** Continue on the boardwalk another 0.3 mile to its end point before turning back.)
- **2.0** Arrive back at the trailhead.

Note: This trail is easy to find and access from numerous points along Moonstone Beach Drive, though it officially starts in the north at the Leffingwell Landing Boat Launch parking area.

4 CAL POLY ARCHITECTURE CANYON

Venture alongside scenic Poly Canyon while enjoying the intermittent shade of eucalyptus and overhanging oaks and sycamore. Then pass beneath a Seuss-like stone arch, and begin exploring the weird and wonderful "architectural graveyard" of experimental structures. Beginning in the 1960s, Cal Poly's Architecture and Environmental Design students were encouraged to embrace the school's motto of "Learn by doing!" by creating and occupying their dwellings for a time. Though the site and projects were, for the most part, abandoned in recent years, hikers can still explore the hillside trails and structures for a unique hiking experience in the hills behind Cal Poly.

Start: At the gated service road entrance for Poly Canyon Road at Village Drive
Elevation gain: 233 feet
Distance: 2.5-mile lollipop, or more as you customize your course
Difficulty: Easy to moderate
Hiking time: About 1 hour 10 minutes
Ages on foot: 4 years+
Seasons/schedule: Year-round, but avoid in hot weather
Fees: Cal Poly has free parking on weekends. Weekdays you will need to purchase a permit to park on campus or use a metered parking space ($–$$).
Trail contact: Cal Poly Visitor Information Center, Grand Avenue, San Luis Obispo 93405, (805) 756-1111
Trail surface: Dirt

Land status: University-owned
Nearest town: San Luis Obispo
Dogs: Yes, on leash
Toilets: Not on trail; try restrooms at campus common areas
Maps: Don't miss the petroglyph-like wooden map to the architecture at the arch
Other trail users: Mountain bikers, joggers, equestrians
Special considerations: Mountain lions are present and frequently spotted in this open space; stay on established trails to avoid poison oak. No longer under the watch of a resident caretaker, some structures suffer from vandalism and graffiti. Though there are occasional clean-up efforts, be mindful when bringing along your literate children of sensitive ages.

FINDING THE TRAILHEAD

From Atascadero, take US 101 south to exit 204. Go left (west) onto Loomis Street for 3 blocks, then turn right (north) onto Grand Avenue. From Pismo Beach, take US 101 north to exit 203D for Grand Avenue. Continue northeast on Grand Avenue as it becomes Perimeter Road for 1 mile before making a right turn onto Village Drive and an immediate left into the H4 Parking Lot (or find nearby street parking). Parking is free on weekends; Mon through Fri use a metered space or get a paid visitors permit at the lot pay station. From here, walk about 0.1 mile farther up Village Drive (north) and turn right (north again) at the poorly labeled, dirt Poly Canyon Road you'll see just before the bright blue emergency help kiosk and Plant Conservatory building. The hike begins at the bright yellow gate crossing Poly Canyon Road. **GPS:** N35 18.26' / W120 39'

THE HIKE

Start at the yellow gate crossing the service road with a modest, metal Poly Canyon sign on your left. Continue around the gate, where the pavement becomes a dirt road.

From here, you'll wander in and out of the shade of oaks lining the relatively flat road, with glimpses of Cal Poly student apartments in the distance and the Brizzolara Creek below to your left as you leave the campus world behind. Keep an eye out for wildlife here, as it's not uncommon to see hawks and even mountain lions from this trail.

At 0.7 mile you'll see a beautiful picnic site to your left shaded by sprawling old oaks, and just ahead to your right, you'll see a cement bench and a small-scale suspension bridge crying out for young kids to explore.

When ready, continue just a tad farther until 0.8 mile where you'll see the unmistakable stone entry arch at the signed entrance to the Architecture Canyon. Bonus points: See if you can spot the terra cotta faces of the arch's creators hidden among its serpentine stones. Then pass through the tightly curving stonework. Cross over the well-shaded Techite Bridge, which is not the cement it looks like, but a fiber-reinforced plastic mortar created by civil engineering students.

As the trees open up, watch for more student structures to appear to your right (east) in the open field, including the reimagined Blade Structure. The original Blade Structure was the first created in the canyon, a project that tested post-tensioning methods along with the use of pre-stressed concrete. After decades of weather and the possible strain of visitors climbing on it and grazing cattle rubbing against it, the Blade Structure literally fell into disrepair. But in 2003, a new team of students redesigned the structure using updated information and new materials—and with the help of three alumni who worked on the original project, the new Blade Structure took shape.

The reinvented Blade Structure greets visitors to the "architectural graveyard" of California Polytechnic State University in the hills of San Luis Obispo.

Top: The Gumby-esque Hay Bale Arch experimented with the use of straw in construction—a surprisingly durable, fantastically insulating, and unquestionably cheap building material.
Bottom: The Cantilever Deck was cleverly designed so that none of the actual structure touches the ground.

At 0.9 mile you'll see a small bridge and massive sycamore to your left and a shady picnic area just beyond in case you brought your lunch or care to stop for a snack. If not, continue straight with the massive, 50-foot Geodesic Dome structure appearing on your right. Built in 1957 by Cal Poly students inspired by a lecture given by legendary architect Buckminster Fuller, this was one of the first geodesic dome structures of its kind built on the west coast. It originally stood on display before the architecture building. Take the left fork here and start uphill toward the Greenhouse, with its three chimney-like stack ventilators, and the Hay Bale Arch visible just above.

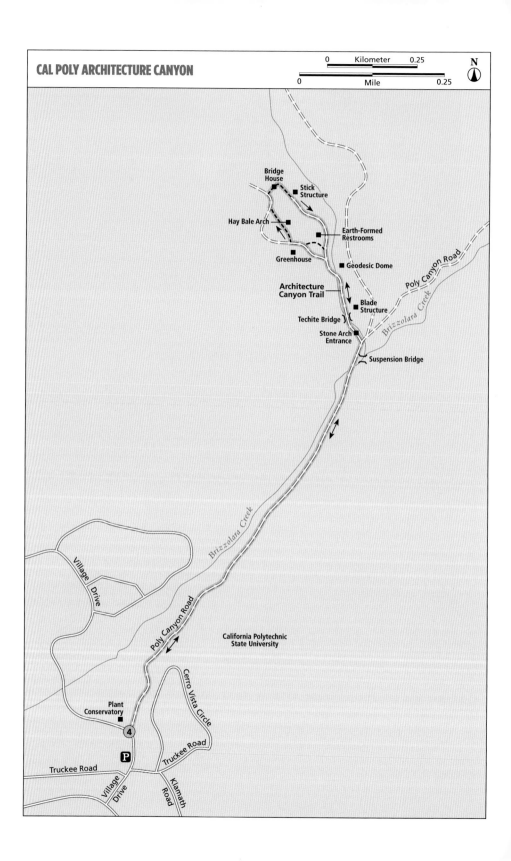

The whimsical stone arch marking the entrance to the Architecture Canyon.

From here, the trails meander at whim to and around the remaining structures, inviting you to do the same (or follow my cues below for a formal lollipop). Explore as you like with a possible visit up at the top to the first permanent addition to the collection in several years: Poly Canyon Observation Deck. Created by students in 2019, the redwood structure was built to give a shady spot for hikers and bikers to rest while enjoying the views—with the hopes of also encouraging others to return to the area and revive interest in the historic site and its potential for future design and architecture students.

When you've finished exploring the hillside, retrace your steps back to Poly Canyon Road and the trailhead.

MILES AND DIRECTIONS

Note: Once you arrive at the Architecture Canyon, the area can be explored by assorted informal trails, crisscrossing through the remaining structures. Here is a suggestion for a simple clockwise route, but feel free to improvise.

0.0 Start at the yellow gate crossing Poly Canyon Road (service road).

0.7 Continue straight on Poly Canyon Road, past a shaded picnic table and small suspension bridge.

0.8 Go toward the left (northwest) to pass beneath the stone arch entrance; continue over the footbridge and watch for the first structures to appear on your right (northeast).

0.9 Arrive at the Geodesic Dome structure and take the left-most of three trails (west) to proceed uphill.

1.1 Continue uphill following the informal trail, then right (northeast) to walk through Bridge House. Follow the trail to the right (southeast) and downhill from the other side.

1.2 Arrive at Stick Structure; continue following the path downhill past Earth-Formed Restrooms (not functional).

1.3 Rejoin earlier trail and trace your steps back to Poly Canyon Road and the yellow gate.

2.5 Arrive back at the yellow gate.

5 EL MORO ELFIN FOREST

This preschooler-approved adventure leads through a fanciful forest of sprawling kid-sized oaks draped in lichen. Native plants and flowers flourish throughout, as a clearly marked boardwalk path keeps you all on track—and out of the brush! Lookouts also give a spectacular view over Morro Bay.

Start: At the 11th Street entrance
Elevation gain: 82 feet
Distance: 1.3-mile loop with spurs
Difficulty: Easy
Hiking time: About 40 minutes
Ages on foot: 2 years+
Seasons/schedule: Open daily sunrise to sunset
Fees: Free
Trail contact: Friends of El Moro Elfin Forest, (805) 528-0392, info@elfin-forest.org, www.elfin-forest.org
Trail surface: Boardwalk for main trail with sand trail offshoots
Land status: Small Wilderness Area Preservation

Nearest town: Los Osos
Dogs: Yes, on leashes no longer than 6 feet
Toilets: None
Maps: Overview maps and parking guide on website. A map is also posted with the informational sign at the 11th Street entrance.
Special considerations: This trail is stroller- and wheelchair-accessible (use 16th Street entrance for ADA-accessible entrance). Coyotes are sometimes present here, so keep dogs close and on leash.

FINDING THE TRAILHEAD

From CA 101 at San Luis Obispo, drive northwest on CA 1 North / Santa Rosa Street for 10.2 miles. Turn left (south) onto San Bernardo Creek Road, which immediately becomes Quintana Road. In 1 mile turn left (south) onto South Bay Boulevard and continue for 2.4 miles. Turn right onto Santa Ysabel Venue, and drive 0.4 mile to 11th Street. (If you prefer to start at the wheelchair-friendly trailhead, turn down 16th Street to enter from there.) Turn right onto 11th Street and park at the end near the Elfin Forest welcome sign and marked trailhead. **GPS:** N35 19.8' / W118 57.6'

THE HIKE

At the end of 11th Street, look for the welcome sign and pass through the wooden railings beside it onto the trail of soft, dark sand. Stay left as the brush rises quickly overhead on both sides, giving a maze-like feel to the forest.

At 0.1 mile you'll get your first Morro Bay view from the preserve, and at 0.2 mile, a small step up puts you onto the boardwalk, with the Bush Lupine Point to your left. Be sure to walk out to enjoy the view from this sleepy side of Morro Bay with Morro Dunes Natural Preserve across the water. An informational sign tells about the Chumash people who returned to the Elfin Forest each spring to fish and collect shellfish a thousand years ago.

At 0.3 mile take the boardwalk to your left (north) and stay left again where the pathway (marked by a sign on the edge of the boardwalk itself) leads out to one of the loveliest viewpoints of all: Siena's View. When ready, retrace your steps back to the boardwalk loop and continue inland (east) with views of the hills and rocky-topped Hollister Peak.

Strolling the Elfin Forest boardwalk with Morro Rock in the distance.

Along this stretch the "pygmy oaks" begin to reveal themselves with glimpses into their sprawling structures that would grow to 50 feet in height elsewhere. But in this harsh, saline soil, the coastal live oaks top out between a mere 4 and 20 feet, though they are more than 100 years old.

At 0.6 mile you'll see the marker for Rose's Grove—not to be missed. Follow the boardwalk path that splits to your right (south) and takes you inside a sheltering pygmy grove with tiny oaks on all sides and their low canopy overhead. It's a wonderful place to stop, take a break on the benches provided here, and soak up the peacefulness of the Elfin Forest.

Return to the main boardwalk and continue to your right (east) following the main path clockwise as it slowly rises to the highest viewpoint, where you can look out over the top of the Elfin Forest to the bay. From here you'll see spur trails leading to the other numbered street entrances, but you will continue on your clockwise route, now heading

Top: Enjoy the magic of Rose's Grove, enclosed by pygmy oak trees.
Bottom: Follow the El Moro Elfin Forest boardwalk inland with Hollister Peak in the distance.

west on the section called The Ridge Trail until at 1.1 miles you see the sandy spur trail marked "11th, 12th, and 13th Street Ends." Turn left (south).

When you come to the unmarked three-way split in the trail, be sure to take a hard right—almost heading back toward Bush Lupine Point. At 1.2 miles you'll take a final left (south) and follow the trail on out to your 11th Street starting point.

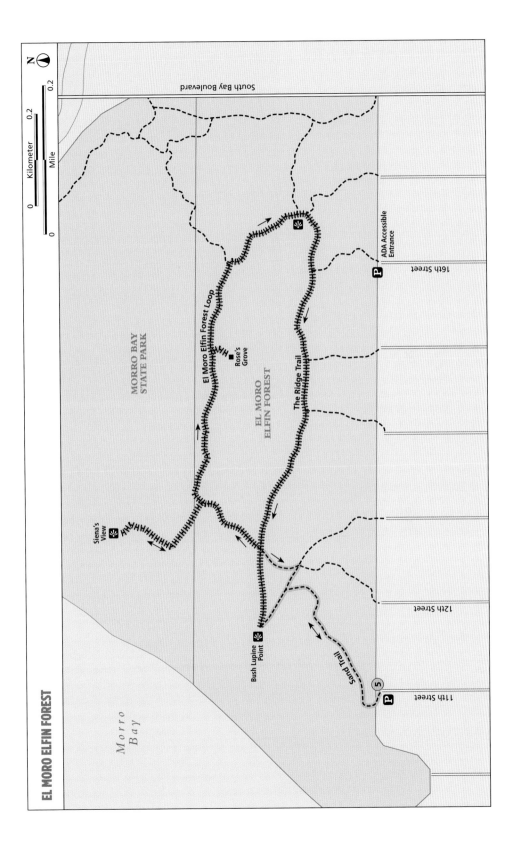

EL MORO ELFIN FOREST

Morro Bay

MORRO BAY STATE PARK

EL MORO ELFIN FOREST

Siena's View

Bush Lupine Point

Rose's Grove

El Moro Elfin Forest Loop

The Ridge Trail

Sand Trail

ADA Accessible Entrance

16th Street

12th Street

11th Street

South Bay Boulevard

N

0   Kilometer   0.2

0   Mile   0.2

MILES AND DIRECTIONS

0.0 Start at the 11th Street entrance and signed trailhead.

0.2 Go left (west) onto the board-walk to Bush Lupine Point, then east along the boardwalk.

0.3 Turn left (north) at the memorial benches, then left again (northwest) at the sign to Siena's View.

0.4 Arrive at Siena's View; back-track to the boardwalk and continue clockwise.

0.6 Take a right (south) into Rose's Grove, then return to the boardwalk, continuing clockwise.

0.8 Arrive at the overlook view-point, continue west on board-walk toward the water.

1.1 Take left (south) sand trail marked "11th, 12th, and 13th Street Ends," and take a hard right (northwest) at the three-way split to follow.

1.3 Turn left (southwest) at the fork to return to the 11th Street trailhead.

A fuchsia-flowering gooseberry is one of many native plants identified along the Elfin Forest trail.

Note: For the best views overall, especially from the gently sloping Ridge Trail, be sure to follow the trail clockwise.

6 MONTAÑA DE ORO BLUFF TRAIL

Montaña de Oro State Park encompasses 8,000 acres of open space between Morro Bay and Pismo Beach at the heart of California's Central Coast. Its 7 miles of protected shoreline include picturesque cliffs, thriving coastal waters, and pristine coves. And there's no better introduction to this park than a hike along the Bluff Trail—particularly in spring when the area pops with the wildflowers that inspired its name: "Mountain of Gold." Better yet, time your hike with low tide for access to vast expanses of tide pools.

Start: At the "Bluff Trail" sign at the first parking area after entering the park
Elevation gain: 115 feet
Distance: 2.4-mile out-and-back (with extension to 4.1 miles)
Difficulty: Easy
Hiking time: About 1.5 hours (allow more if tide pooling or picnicking)
Ages on foot: 4 years+
Seasons/schedule: Open daily 6 a.m. to 10 p.m.; for tide pool access, check low tide times for "Spooners Cove" at www.tideschart.com
Fees: State park day-use fee ($$) or California Explorer Pass
Trail contact: California State Parks, 3550 Pecho Valley Rd., Los Osos 93402, (805) 772-6101
Trail surface: Gravel, sand, and dirt

Land status: State park
Nearest town: Los Osos
Dogs: No dogs on trails or beaches (except Spooner's Cove beach)
Toilets: At Spooner Ranch House and just east of bridge crossing
Maps: Visit website for overview maps and parking guide.
Other trail users: Mountain bikers on main path/service road
Special considerations: Steep cliffs with no railing (alternatively you can avoid the trails closest to the cliff edges in these areas by staying on the main trail/service road) and the usual ocean concerns in tide pooling areas. Check conditions before your visit and always tide pool with caution!

FINDING THE TRAILHEAD

From San Luis Obispo, take Los Osos Valley Road west for 8.4 miles. Continue as it becomes Pecho Valley Road, arriving at Montaña de Oro State Park in 3 miles, and then continue another 0.7 mile (past the Spooner Ranch House and Visitor Center) to the Bluff Trail parking area on the right (west) side of the road. Additional parking is available just ahead at the Valencia Peak trailhead on the opposite side of the road. The signed Bluff Trail begins at the southwest end of the Bluff Trail parking area. **GPS:** N35 16.32' / W120 53.28'

THE HIKE

As you set out from the signed trailhead near the historic Spooner Ranch House and Visitor Center, stay right as the trail forks at 0.1 mile and views quickly open up over Spooner's Cove. In another 0.1 mile you'll pass remnants of a cement foundation near the cliff's edge. Here, the enterprising Spooner family solved the problem of transporting products from their ranchland, which had virtually no road access, to profitable markets.

This unlikely, cliff-top location became the site of a warehouse and a lengthy chute dug *through* the cliff that enabled them to load their products—milk, butter, and even live

View from the south side of Spooner's Cove toward the Pacific

Top: A great egret fishes in the rocky tidepools at Montaña de Oro State Park.
Bottom: Exploring tide pools in the exposed shale shelves at Quarry Cove.

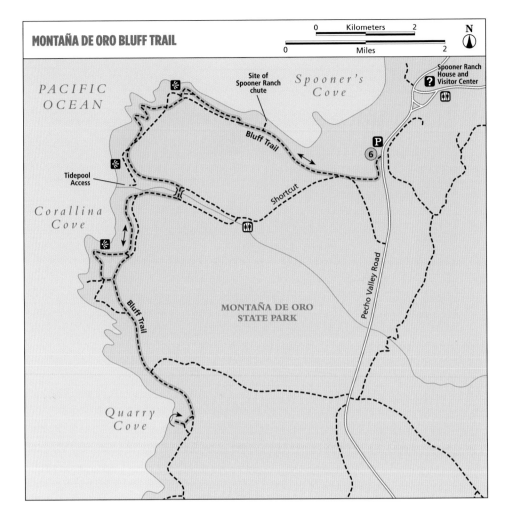

PACIFIC OCEAN

Spooner Ranch House and Visitor Center

Site of Spooner Ranch chute

Spooner's Cove

Bluff Trail

Tidepool Access

Corallina Cove

Shortcut

Pecho Valley Road

MONTAÑA DE ORO STATE PARK

Bluff Trail

Quarry Cove

pigs—from the bluff onto schooners traveling up the coast to San Francisco and other large markets along the coastline.

Continuing west toward the Pacific, take care to stay on the established dirt trail and avoid the eroding cliff edge. At times, you'll see the trail split with one route following nearer the edge or splitting off to scenic spurs and one a little farther inland for those who prefer it (e.g., those hiking with a young child or predisposed to a fear of heights).

At 0.4 mile you'll reach the west-most point below Spooner's Cove, where a bench overlooks the cove and the Pacific. Look for tall, sleek cormorants and red-eyed, red-billed black oystercatchers resting on the rocky islets. You may also spot black and white pigeon guillemots bobbing and diving from the ocean's surface, followed by flashes of their bright red feet.

This area falls right in the middle of the Pacific Flyway and is considered one of the best birding spots in all of California. Better still, all the exposed rocks, reefs, and land features you can see within 12 nautical miles of shore are part of the California Coastal

National Monument, making it an important resting and nesting zone for coastal birds of all kinds.

From here, the Bluff Trail continues south, overlooking rugged marine terraces of exposed shale dating back 5 to 6 million years. These layers of ancient ocean floor have been thrust up over time by the tectonic forces at work along this edge of the Pacific Plate.

At 0.6 mile you'll arrive at the Corallina Cove Overlook, where an adjacent stairway gives access to excellent tide pooling at low tides. If you venture out to this rocky reef (or any others along the trail), take extra care with where you step to avoid crushing critters that may cling to any part of the surfaces here (not just well-defined pools), and always keep an eye on the unpredictable waves.

After turning briefly inland for a bridge crossing over a narrow, nasturtium-filled canyon, the trail leads back out toward the Pacific and the next scenic viewpoint at 0.9 mile. In addition to excellent birdwatching, Montaña de Oro offers some of the best opportunities along the west coast to view marine mammals from shore. Like the Moonstone Beach Boardwalk, it's a stop on the official Whale Trail and offers year-round opportunities to see multiple whale species, dolphins, sea otters, elephant seals, harbor seals, and sea lions.

Continue south another 0.75 mile to arrive at Quarry Cove, where two picnic tables overlook an especially rugged, rocky tidal zone. This is a great spot to enjoy a picnic lunch and additional tide pooling before retracing your steps back to the trailhead. If needed, take the Bluff Trail shortcut with restrooms on your return (see map.)

MILES AND DIRECTIONS

0.0   Start at the trailhead.

0.1   Stay right (west) at the fork.

0.2   Arrive at the site of Spooner Ranch loading chute.

0.4   Reach the first viewpoint with a bench.

0.6   Arrive at Corallina Cove and tide pool access.

0.7   Cross the bridge.

0.9   Come to the Whale Trail viewpoint.

1.2   Arrive at Quarry Cove; backtrack when ready.

2.4   Return to the trailhead.

7 PISMO BOARDWALK, BUTTERFLIES, AND BEACH

This leisurely hike combines a boardwalk stroll with elevated spans above ice plant–clad, mini dunes with a visit to a eucalyptus grove populated by possibly thousands of monarch butterflies, and it ends with a romp on a sweeping Central Coast beach. Bring a picnic—and possibly a kite!

Start: At the unassuming trailhead with "dogs on leash only" sign directly behind the restrooms
Elevation gain: 13 feet
Distance: 1.6 miles
Difficulty: Easy
Hiking time: About 1 hour
Ages on foot: 2 years+
Seasons/schedule: Open daily sunrise to sunset, but monarchs are best seen Nov through Feb
Fees: Free
Trail contact: Central Coast State Parks Association, 555 Pier Ave., Oceano 93445, (805) 473-7220
Trail surface: Boardwalk and sand
Land status: State beach
Nearest town: Grover Beach

Dogs: Yes, on leash
Toilets: Yes, flush toilets at trailhead and chemical toilets at monarch grove
Maps: No official map, use the one included in the chapter
Gear suggestions: Binoculars and a good zoom lens for viewing and photographing the butterflies; an extra pair of dry shoes for after the hike in case yours get wet while crossing the mini lagoons to the beach!
Special considerations: The boardwalk trail and grove are stroller- and wheelchair-accessible and have benches for resting along the way.

FINDING THE TRAILHEAD

From CA 1 / Pacific Boulevard at Grover Beach, drive west on West Grand Avenue 0.2 mile following signs for coastal access. Take a short right at Dune Trail, then left, and begin looking for your parking space in the large, free parking area. The trailhead is behind the restrooms and picnic area opposite Fin's Restaurant. **GPS:** N35 7.39' / W12 38.0'

THE HIKE

Make your way onto the boardwalk trail up and over the mounds of pretty (although invasive) ice plant sprawling over mini sand dunes on both sides of you. As the path ramps up, look west and enjoy glimpses of the ocean above the sandy hillocks (great photo ops!).

When the boardwalk ends, stay to the right, following the wider sand path inland toward the campground and alongside Meadow Creek. Cross the first bridge over the creek and continue toward the large grove of eucalyptus, then take the narrow metal bridge to your right back over the creek and into the grove. Here the trail zigzags around the first of the trees and then passes through the heart of the grove. Watch for sandwich board signs placed to help direct you to the best butterfly clusters during your visit, and *look up!*

A magnificent cluster of wintering Monarch butterflies clings to a eucalyptus bough in the Pismo State Beach Monarch Butterfly Grove.

During the months of November through February, monarchs "overwinter" here, clinging in big, protective clusters high in the boughs of the eucalyptus. They can be tricky to see at first—with the outer sides of their wings blending well with the leaves of the eucalyptus (especially in the lighting within the grove).

Top: Exploring the boardwalk path flanked by ice plant en route to the monarch grove.
Bottom: As the tide recedes, this stretch of beach can become a magical mirror.

But watch—and you might begin to see the butterflies flitting in or out from the clusters and their flashes of bright orange wings occasionally opening as they rest in the trees. And why shouldn't they rest? These monarchs may have flown 1,000 miles to get here from as far away as Canada, sometimes flying as much as 50 to 100 miles in a day and at heights of up to 900 stories in the air!

Continue following the path through the grove and look for the information board where, in butterfly season, you may see the day's estimated count for monarchs presently in the grove.

As you exit the grove where you entered, continue on the sand path straight toward the small, tree-topped sand dune with the powdery light sand and small sandy dunes

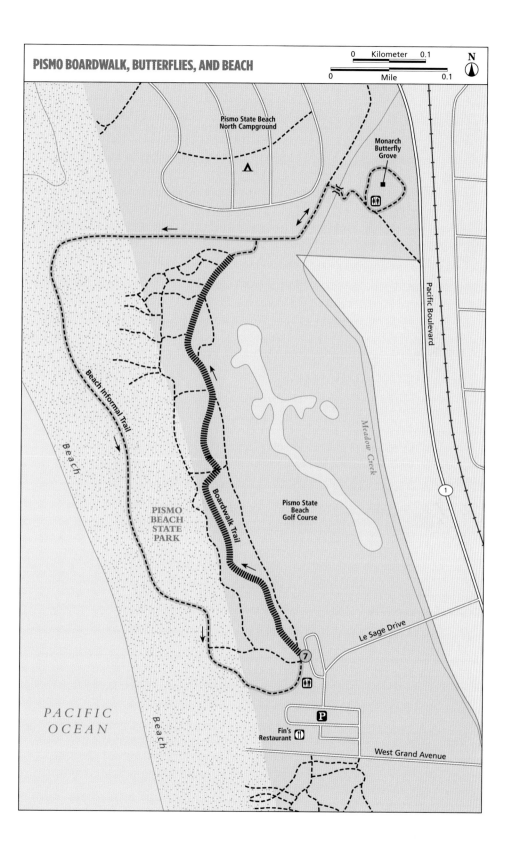

PISMO BOARDWALK, BUTTERFLIES, AND BEACH

Kilometer

Mile

N

Pismo State Beach
North Campground

Monarch
Butterfly
Grove

Beach Informal Trail

Beach

Meadow Creek

Pacific Boulevard

PISMO
BEACH
STATE
PARK

Boardwalk Trail

Pismo State
Beach
Golf Course

1

Le Sage Drive

7

PACIFIC
OCEAN

Beach

P

Fin's
Restaurant

West Grand Avenue

rolling just beyond, between you and the Pacific. Meadow Creek meanders through here, and you will need to cross it either by wading or looking for the narrowest place you can find (look for where other beachgoers may have built a sand dam or placed a large piece of driftwood across).

Continue forward onto the beach and return southward at your leisure. Watch for the many different-patterned clam shells you might see along the way, thanks to the sandpipers who feast on the bivalves beneath the sand. Curious kids may enjoy looking for the "sand bubbles" forming where air rises through the sand above active clams and digging down until they find the live clams. When placed on top of the sand, the clams begin vanishing sideways into the sand!

As you make your return journey along the beach, watch for Fin's Restaurant and the small wooden overlook to your left (east) just before it. The wooden overlook marks the beach access path back to the restrooms and parking area where you started.

MILES AND DIRECTIONS

- 0.0   Start at the trailhead behind restrooms.
- 0.5   As the boardwalk ends, turn right (east) on the path and follow northeast along the creek.
- 0.6   Veer right at footbridge to enter the eucalyptus grove; follow the path counterclockwise.
- 0.8   Exit the grove at the same bridge; backtrack along the path toward the boardwalk.
- 0.9   Continue straight (west) to the end of the path and onto the beach.
- 1.0   Walk south along the beach.
- 1.5   Exit the beach at the mini boardwalk toward restrooms.
- 1.6   Arrive back where you started.

Note: You can start this loop at the monarch grove instead; however, parking there is extremely limited and many visitors end up walking along the busy road to get to the entrance. As written, you'll have the benefit of abundant free parking and the better restrooms to start and end your hike—and it's much more pleasant to enter the monarch grove from the footbridge side rather than the street.

8 GOLETA BEACH AND UCSB LAGOON

Enjoy a leisurely journey from busy beach park to wide, sweeping beach, to peaceful lagoon paths, and finally the beautifully land-scaped campus of UC Santa Barbara (UCSB). This easy hike is best at low tide when you can include a long stretch of beach along the south and western portions of UCSB. When the tide is in, just continue along the campus perimeter trail above the Pacific instead of going down to the beach. There are many benches to rest at and opportunities to access beaches for picnicking or playing along the way.

Start: Dirt trail at west end of Goleta Beach parking area (parallel to busy bicycle path)
Elevation gain: 157 feet
Distance: 3.4-mile lollipop
Difficulty: Easy
Hiking time: About 1 hour 45 minutes
Ages on foot: 3 years+
Seasons/schedule: Year-round, but to include the beach portion, you must hike at low tide. Check the tides for Campus Point Beach, Santa Barbara County, at www.tideschart .com.
Fees: No fees or permits required when parking at Goleta Beach

Trail contact: UC Santa Barbara, Santa Barbara 93106, (805) 893-8000
Trail surface: Paved, dirt, sand, rock
Land status: County park and university-owned
Nearest town: Goleta and Isla Vista
Dogs: Yes, on leash
Toilets: At Goleta Beach
Maps: See (and print) a detailed map of the UCSB Campus Lagoon Area Restoration Trails with an overview of the ongoing restoration projects you'll pass by at www.ccber.ucsb.edu
Special considerations: Ocean

FINDING THE TRAILHEAD

From US 101/CA 1, take exit 104B onto CA 217 for the Airport/UCSB. In 0.2 mile, continue on CA 217/Ward Memorial Boulevard 1.8 miles to exit 1 for Sandspit Road. Turn left (south) onto Sandspit Road Goleta Beach Park, then turn right (south) to stay on Sandspit Road as it delivers you to the Goleta Beach County Park parking area. The trail begins at the west end of the parking area. **GPS:** N34 25.95' / W119 50.17'

THE HIKE

The hike begins at the west end of the parking lot, where an informal dirt trail traces the low bluff as the beach recedes. Though an established bike path runs almost parallel to this, families (especially with young kids) will find the less busy footpath preferable.

After passing the Henley Gate entrance to UC Santa Barbara (0.1 mile), the pedestrian pathway turns to packed sand and climbs very gradually, with benches overlooking the water along the way.

At 0.6 mile, as you arrive at a small, paid campus parking lot, look left (east) for the wooden fencing with three sure signs of adventure marking the top of the stairs to the

The view of UC Santa Barbara from "the island" of the lagoon.

beach: Tsunami Hazard Zone, Falling Rocks, and DANGER: Unstable Bluffs. Take a look out over the beach from here to confirm the tide is out and you have plenty of sand (and distance from the palm-topped bluffs) to stroll. If so, make your way down the stairs to continue your journey south along the beach. (If not, continue south along this upper trail toward Campus Point.)

At about 1 mile you'll turn inland to rejoin the main campus path up the steps to the wooden Campus Point multilevel overlook. But, depending on the tide conditions, you may have some interesting tide pools to explore before doing so.

Once you reach the top of the steps, take the left-most trail (east) to follow along the informal trails nearest the water to the south-most point and then turning right (west) for the best views over the ocean. Here you'll begin to see signs of UCSB's various restoration projects past and present, including current efforts to replace invasive ice plant with native dune and coastal scrub vegetation.

At 1.4 miles, you'll see a large interpretive sign with photos and the names of many of the flowering plants you may see on your visit, such as seacliff daisy, beach evening primrose, heliotrope, and seaside fiddleneck. A sandy trail leads from the sign to a small, quiet beach in case you are ready for a midhike picnic.

From here, you will continue on the main path just 0.1 mile farther to where a dirt singletrack darts off to the right (northeast) and begins the journey around what some call "the island" of the lagoon. As you gain elevation above the water, watch for egrets, heron, and cormorants, all of which frequent the lagoon and flock to the peaceful trees and snags at the water's edge around the island.

As you complete your island excursion, the path gradually descends until you rejoin the main path (partly paved here) and continue east, just briefly. At 2.1 miles take the packed-sand path at the lagoon's edge north toward the campus buildings until it becomes sidewalk along the north side of the lagoon. At 2.5 miles cross the road and take the cement stairs heading northward to the campus buildings and toward Storke Tower, the landmark 175-foot bell tower on the UCSB campus completed in 1969.

You'll pass by the university's colorful art building, art museum, and the sunken Storke Plaza koi pond before reaching Storke Tower itself at 2.6 miles. Here you'll turn right in front of the tower and continue east on pedestrian walkways for 0.2 mile, before turning left (north) at the wide paved open space with picnic tables to each side and the sprawling Davidson Library on your right (east).

Explore a beautiful sweeping beach that appears only when the tide is out.

When you reach the north end of the library complex, turn right (east) and follow the paved walkways east toward the Engineering II building at the far end, as the network of sidewalks sprawls through grassy lawn and inviting shade trees. If you notice the trees getting more interesting as you go, that's because the grounds of the UCSB campus itself are considered a "living classroom," with more than 250 tree species from six continents. (If visiting in spring, prepare to be dazzled by the scarlet blossom canopies of the coral trees!)

Pass through the open Engineering II corridor, continuing east until you arrive at the crosswalk at Lagoon Road. Once across, retrace your steps on the pedestrian path beside the ocean back to the trailhead.

TIMELY TUNES

UC Santa Barbara's Storke Tower is a campanile (bell and clock tower) featuring sixty-one bells weighing from 13 to 4,793 pounds each. It's named for the Pulitzer Prize–winning journalist, Thomas M. Storke, who contributed generously to the building of the tower and the Storke Communications Plaza below, which houses the university newspaper, a radio station, and the yearbook office at the base of this tower. Listen for the bells at the start of the hour when they play the Westminster Quarters— or sometimes a surprise tune by UCSB students or special visitors.

GOLETA BEACH AND UCSB LAGOON

MILES AND DIRECTIONS

0.0   Start on the informal dirt trail at the west end of the parking area.

0.1   Continue on the trail beside the road as it passes through Henley Gate.

0.6   When the tide is out, take the wooden stairs down to the beach beside the paid parking area (if tide is in, continue on trail above).

1.0   Turn inland (northwest) and reconnect with the campus trail.

1.1   Climb Campus Point stairs; at top take left-most trail for bluff's edge.

1.3   Take right fork (north) toward the lagoon.

1.5   Take right (northeast) singletrack dirt path (or alternatively skip this island adventure and continue on the main lagoon path).

1.6   As you reach the first point, go left (northwest) to continue along the lagoon.

2.0   Rejoin the main trail (partially paved here).

Completing our trip around "the island" at the heart of the serene Campus Lagoon.

2.1 Take a hard right (north) onto the packed-sand path along the lagoon's edge toward campus.

2.4 The lagoon path ends; follow the road to the right (east) briefly and cross to the stairs going up toward the bell tower.

2.6 Turn right (west) in front of Storke Tower (bell tower).

2.8 Go left (north) through an open space and past the library.

2.9 Turn right (east) past the end of the library complex; continue straight all the way through Engineering II building.

3.2 Cross street at crosswalk; retrace your steps along the path toward Goleta Beach.

3.4 Arrive back at the trailhead.

An informational sign identifies native plants and wildflowers used in restoration projects along the bluff—and the invasive species they seek to replace.

9 DOUGLAS FAMILY PRESERVE BLUFF TRAIL

Dog lovers flock to this off-leash preserve with lofty views over Hendry's Beach and the Santa Barbara Channel, including views of the Channel Islands on clear days. Bring Fido and a picnic to enjoy seated on a log along the way. If you're lucky, paragliders or hang gliders may also be launching from the bluff.

Start: At the green gated entrance to the preserve, west end of Medcliff Road
Elevation gain: 75 feet
Distance: 1-mile out-and-back, or choose your own adventure from an easy network of trails.
Difficulty: Easy
Hiking time: About 45 minutes
Ages on foot: 2 years+ (if comfortable with dogs)
Seasons/schedule: Year-round
Fees: Free
Trail contact: City of Santa Barbara Parks and Recreation, 620 Laguna St., Santa Barbara 93101, (805) 564-5418, SantaBarbaraCA.gov/parks
Trail surface: Dirt

Land status: Open space/nature preserve
Nearest town: Santa Barbara
Maps: Printable Parks and Recreation Map of Santa Barbara at santabarbaraca.gov
Dogs: Yes, dogs can frolic off leash in Douglas Family Preserve and below this trail on the east side of Arroyo Burro Beach (aka Hendry's Beach).
Toilets: No, but restrooms at Arroyo Burro Beach nearby (day-use fee may apply)
Special considerations: Consider your child's comfort level (and your own) with unfamiliar dogs off leash, as there will likely be a few along your route

FINDING THE TRAILHEAD

From US 101 / CA 1, take exit 97 and head southeast onto Castillo Street. In 0.1 mile turn right onto West Montecito Street, then make a slight left (southwest) onto Cliff Drive. Continue 2.1 miles on Cliff Drive, then turn left (south) onto Mesa Lane. In 0.3 mile turn right onto Medcliff Road and begin looking for street parking along this final 0.2 mile. The trailhead is at the west end of Medcliff Road. **GPS:** N34 23.97' / W119 44.08'

THE HIKE

This peaceful, easy hike begins at the Douglas Family Preserve wooden sign and green gate and progresses quite simply along a well-established trail that follows the bluff. While there is a small network of trails to explore, this favored route is out and back at the bluff's edge, enjoying the views over the kelp-rich, vibrant Santa Barbara Channel between windswept trees the whole way.

Just after you enter the preserve, watch for the eucalyptus trees to the east side of the pathway—especially if you're visiting in the winter months when numerous monarchs are most likely to be found overwintering in these trees. During the coolest coastal days, they'll look like dried leaves, dangling from the limbs of the eucalyptus, the bright sides of their wings hidden. But at the end of a warm afternoon, watch as they flock back with their dazzling orange wings to the shelter of these trees.

Enjoying views from the fido-friendly bluff trail at Douglas Family Preserve.

This next stretch is where you might have the pleasure of seeing paragliders with their gracefully arching chutes filled with the updraft breeze as they teeter on the bluff's edge waiting for that just-right moment to launch. Hang gliders also enjoy this location, and with the spectacular views out to the Channel Islands, it's easy to see why.

Continue along the bluff trail, and watch for the dedication stone on your left (west). The stone recognizes the many individuals who helped make it possible to purchase this 70-acre parcel of prime California real estate in 1997 and preserve it for public enjoyment—most notably the Kirk Douglas family for which the preserve has been named.

As you continue northwestward along the bluff trail, you'll see Hendry's Beach coming into view below. This is a nice area to look for a stump or log to sit upon and watch for the varied wildlife that thrives along this zone. Above the water, you may see brown

Top: A paraglider tests the breeze at the Douglas Family Preserve.
Bottom left: The view north with Arroyo Burro County Beach in the distance.
Bottom right: Catching a glimpse of the Channel Islands across the Santa Barbara Channel.

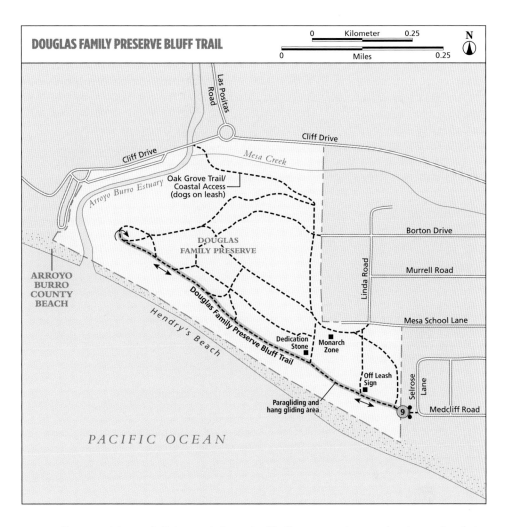

DOUGLAS FAMILY PRESERVE BLUFF TRAIL

Kilometer
0   0.25

Miles
0   0.25

N

Las Positas Road

Cliff Drive

Cliff Drive

Mesa Creek

Arroyo Burro Estuary

Oak Grove Trail/
Coastal Access
(dogs on leash)

Borton Drive

DOUGLAS
FAMILY PRESERVE

Murrell Road

ARROYO
BURRO
COUNTY
BEACH

Linda Road

Mesa School Lane

Hendry's Beach

Douglas Family Preserve Bluff Trail

Dedication
Stone

Monarch
Zone

Off Leash
Sign

Selrose Lane

Paragliding and
hang gliding area

9   Medcliff Road

PACIFIC OCEAN

pelicans cruising and diving, and along the bluff you may also spot hawks soaring (who also favor the eucalyptus in the preserve). But out in the nutrient-rich channel is a busy world where dolphin and humpback whale sightings are a regular occurrence.

The flat trail continues along the bluff until reaching a pleasant lookout point over Hendry's Beach and the bustling Arroyo Burro County Beach (keep kids and pets close as there is no defined edge or railing). When ready, turn back and retrace your leisurely steps along the bluff trail.

MILES AND DIRECTIONS

0.0   Start at the green gate beside the Douglas Family Preserve sign.

0.1   Pass the "Dogs Off Leash" sign.

0.5   Arrive at the end point of Bluff Trail; reverse course.

1.0   Return to the trailhead.

10 SADDLE ROCK TRAIL

Start with a gradual climb from a lovely neighborhood in the Montecito Hills through shady oaks and thriving native plants down the popular Hot Springs Trail. Then turn up the Saddle Rock Trail with a bridge-less creek crossing and cardio climb up through sandstone boulders to views of the Pacific—and the northern Channel Islands on clear days—until you reach the landmark Saddle Rock. Connecting trails make it easy to add on to your out-and-back hike or form loops.

Start: Hot Springs trailhead on East Mountain Road near Riven Rock Road
Elevation gain: 472 feet
Distance: 1.8-mile out-and-back
Difficulty: Moderate to strenuous because of big, uneven rocky steps and a steep climb up the last stretch (an extra workout for little legs)
Hiking time: About 1 hour
Ages on foot: 5 years+
Seasons/schedule: Year-round, but be mindful of heat on the exposed upper section and start early
Fees: Free
Trail contact: Montecito Trails Foundation, PO Box 5481, Santa Barbara 93150, (805) 969-3514, www.montecitotrailsfoundation

.info; Los Padres National Forest, Santa Barbara Ranger District, 3505 Paradise Rd., Santa Barbara 93105, (805) 448-3648, www.fs.usda.gov/detail/lpnf/
Trail surface: Dirt and rock
Land status: National forest
Nearest town: Montecito
Toilets: None
Dogs: Yes, on leash
Maps: See trail map displayed at information kiosk as you begin at Hot Springs Trail.
Special considerations: Watch out for poison oak along narrow sections of trail; mountain bikers and equestrians also use the Hot Springs Trail portion of this hike

FINDING THE TRAILHEAD

From US 101, take exit 94A for Olive Mill Road, driving north (away from the ocean here) for 0.5 mile and continuing straight as it becomes Hot Springs Road. In another 1.3 miles, turn left (east) onto East Mountain Drive. In 0.2 mile you'll see the small parking area by the signed trailhead on your right (north). If these spaces are full, look for nose-in parking along the shoulder of Riven Rock Road heading south from here (watch out for soft dirt!). **GPS:** N34 26.9' / W119 38.8'

THE HIKE

The hike begins at the tumble of purple trumpet vine to the right (east) end of the parking area, with the wooden Hot Springs Trail sign. Pass through a narrow stretch with fencing (and private property) on both sides. Soon the pathway opens wider beneath the shade of coastal live oak, and at 50 yards in, you'll see the Hot Springs Trail information kiosk with an overview map of the local trails (snap a phone photo to keep it on hand if needed).

Follow the trail signs as they guide you briefly alongside the quiet, residential Hot Springs Road with boulders and arching oak trees separating the path from pavement. At 0.3 mile, where you see a gate crossing the road, follow the "Trail" sign to continue on

The steep climb is rewarded by glorious views over the Pacific, sometimes to the Channel Islands.

the dirt path to the right of the gate. Here you'll follow along the left side of the lower Hot Springs creek bed (mostly dry, most of the year), where you might have the added bonus of wildflowers and butterfly sightings much of the year.

Soon the trail splits and you'll follow the well-signed right fork for the Saddle Rock Trail as the main Hot Springs Trail continues on the left. Venture down toward the Hot Springs creek bed, where you'll cross atop the large boulders like stepping-stones past either a trickling brook or dry creek depending on the timing of your visit. Once across, the climb begins!

At 0.6 mile you'll take a right (east) up the steep steps marked for Saddle Rock Trail, ignoring the dirt road marked with an old rusty "Private Road" sign, which is now used as part of a loop trail by some Hot Springs Trail hikers. Marvel as the dirt trail steepens yet more, and take care with loose rocks along the way. It won't be long before you glance back to see the lovely view above Montecito.

As the climb continues, watch for the stalwart survivor oak, a magnificent old oak tree that withstood the devastating Thomas Fire that swept through this area in December of 2017, and the mud flow that followed in early 2018. If you're ready to take a water break,

The hike begins in a quiet neighborhood following a wash filled with wildflowers.

you'll find the perfect spot in the shade of this tree with sitting rocks and views to enjoy over the Montecito Hills, Carpinteria, Summerland, and the Santa Barbara Channel.

The steep climb continues, feeling briefly like you're traveling up a chute more than a path, and when it opens up again the view will be all the more impressive. Look out across the water to see if you can spot the Channel Islands. Then take note of the resilient landscape, where verdant vegetation springs back between boulders and even from fire-scarred trees as the hillside reclaims its natural beauty.

Before you know it, the unmistakable Saddle Rock rises up into view. For bouldering enthusiasts, you'll also find many fun and easy challenges in this area. Families that want more of a challenge can continue on up the Saddle Rock Trail to where it intercepts the Edison Catway, then doubles back for a total distance of 2.3 miles and 719-foot elevation gain.

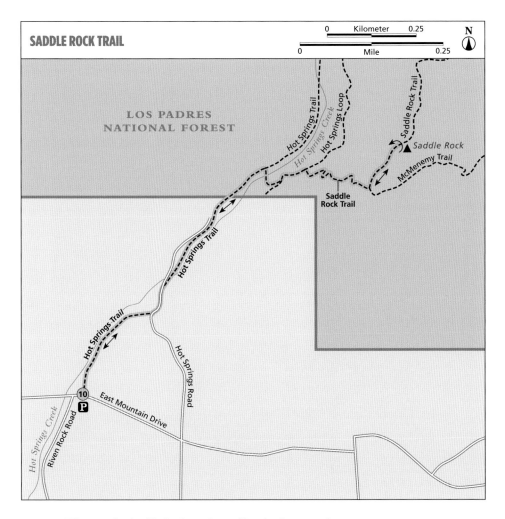

When ready, double back to the trailhead where you began.

MILES AND DIRECTIONS

0.0   Start at Hot Springs Trailhead.

0.2   Continue on the marked trail beside the neighborhood street.

0.3   Walk briefly on the neighborhood road to where the trail continues to the right (west) of gate.

0.5   Take the right fork (south) for Saddle Rock Trail, cross the creek bed, continue up the other side.

0.6   Turn right (southeast) at "Saddle Rock / Girard / San Ysidro Trails" sign and proceed up the steps.

0.8   Take a left (north at fork) and continue up Saddle Rock Trail.

0.9   Arrive at Saddle Rock. Reverse course when ready, enjoying the views.

1.8   Arrive back at the trailhead.

Top: A fire-scarred survivor, this old oak withstood wildfire and continues to offer hikers a shady resting spot with a view.
Bottom: Enjoying the view of—and views from—Saddle Rock.

Side trip: When your kids are ready for an even greater challenge—with an approximate 900-foot elevation gain in only 3.4 miles—take the Saddle Rock Trail all the way up and go right (east) on the Edison Catway to form a loop using the Girard Trail and McMenemy Trail to return to the lower portion of the Saddle Rock Trail. Be sure to consult the overview map of these trails at the information kiosk, and start early—this is not a hike for hot weather!

11 CAVERN POINT LOOP TO POTATO HARBOR

Watch for the cat-sized Channel Island fox as you start your adventure, soon to make a steep but rewarding climb to your first exhilarating view from the wind-swept bluffs of beautiful Santa Cruz Island. Then it's views-views-views of intriguing cliffs and caverns and turquoise coves until at last you arrive at that most spectacular overlook of all: Potato Harbor. When conditions are right, there's no better place for a picnic. Then journey back and pick up the other half of the Cavern Point Loop taking you to your highest point of the trek before returning to Scorpion Harbor.

Start: Scorpion Cove Anchorage
Elevation gain: 551 feet (262 feet Cavern Point Loop)
Distance: 5-mile lollipop (or 2-mile loop)
Difficulty: Moderate
Hiking time: About 2 hours 15 minutes
Ages on foot: 7 years+
Seasons/schedule: Year-round
Fees: There is no entrance fee to visit Channel Islands National Park, but you will need to book transportation to the island through concessionaire Island Packers https://islandpackers .com ($$$$). Infants 0–2 years are free but require a reservation.
Trail contact: Superintendent, Channel Islands National Park, 1901 Spinnaker Dr., Ventura 93001, (805) 658-5730
Trail surface: Dirt, rock, chalk

Land status: National park
Nearest town: Ventura
Dogs: No dogs
Toilets: At Scorpion Anchorage and campground
Maps: See the Santa Cruz Island Hiking Map and Guide at www.NPS. gov/chis/ for reference
Special considerations: Sections of the trail follow along steep cliffs and drop-offs. Though set back from the trail, there are no guard rails here so only bring hikers who will stick to the trail. There are no concessions on the island so be sure to bring all the food and drinks you'll want while on the island. (Potable water is available in the Lower Scorpion Campground.) Bring towels and swimsuits if you'd like to swim before returning to the mainland.

FINDING THE TRAILHEAD

After disembarking your Island Packers ferry at Scorpion Anchorage, proceed straight off the pier toward the first (and busiest) set of restrooms and an information kiosk, and you're already on your way! Look for a ranger or docent greeting fresh arrivals in this area with important information for your visit and departure time. **GPS:** N34 2.95' / W119 33.34'

THE HIKE

The day's adventure begins with a 1-hour ferry ride (or longer if the wildlife is performing) from Ventura Harbor to Scorpion Anchorage on Santa Cruz Island. With any luck, you'll see dolphins leaping at play along the way and possibly other marine mammals that frequent these nutrient–rich waters. In one summer month, all Island Packers vessels combined may report over 50,000 common dolphin sightings alone! Add to that the possibility of glimpsing bottle nose or Risso's dolphins; or minke, humpback, or blue whales; flying fish or a mako shark; and you may be too busy watching at the rails to make use of your seats on the boat.

As you disembark at Scorpion Anchorage, continue straight (west) from the pier toward the first (and busiest) set of vault toilets with changing stalls at each end. You'll find storage lockers (unlocked and shared with fellow travelers) along here where you can stash anything you might not want to carry on the hike but would enjoy afterward (beach towel, small ice chest).

Somewhere along this main "landing strip" for fresh arrivals, you'll find a docent or ranger giving a short talk about the island's history, ranger-led talks, and important things to know like to *never* leave your daypack out of reach as the determinedly dexterous ravens can open them in a blink, and never trust the cunning island foxes with an unzipped tent unless you want an extra roommate.

When ready, continue straight (west) toward the historic Scorpion Ranch house and Visitor Center, and turn left (south), then right (west), to follow along its fence line. Ignore all the day-trippers charging up the hillside at the first Cavern Point Loop trail sign; instead continue past the kayak and snorkel rental shop (rentals must be arranged prior to your visit) and the second, far less busy set of vault toilets.

If you haven't yet spotted an island fox, keep a close eye out. Between here and the campground you're about to walk through is where you're most likely to spot one—or

Potato Harbor on Santa Cruz Island, Channel Islands National Park.

Hikers get their first breathtaking view from Cavern Point Loop.

two or three. As you continue west, look for the main path / dirt service road passing through the Lower Scorpion Campground, where you'll find two potable water taps if you need to top off water bottles, and follow it northwest to the *other* Cavern Point / Potato Harbor trail sign. Here begins the climb!

The trail quickly becomes a steep slant against the hillside, just dirt, loose rocks, and occasional chalky patches as you keep climbing and climbing the next 0.3 mile toward what seems to be only sky. At last—at only 0.6 mile into the hike, you'll reach the first overlook: a jaw-dropping view from the high cliffside across the Scorpion Marine Reserve. To appreciate how far you've already climbed turn around and note the bit of blue ocean you can also see over the other side of the island.

(**Option:** For a shorter hike [2 miles], you can continue on the Cavern Point Loop to your right [northeast] here—but don't expect the climbing to get easier any time soon.) For the full hike and what most visitors feel is the most beautiful viewpoint on the island, turn left here (west) to follow the Potato Overlook / North Bluff Trail.

It's easy to feel on top of the world—and a world away from California—as you hike along this coastal bluff with views over amazing coves of tourmaline waters and vibrant kelp jungles. Lovingly referred to as the "Galapagos of North America," the Channel Islands emerged from the sea some 5 million years ago and were never connected to the mainland. This gave rise to unique animal species like the resident island fox, spotted skunk, island scrub jay, and island deer mouse, as well as dozens of plant species you will find only in these islands—including eight plants that are found only on Santa Cruz Island. Watch for flowering native island plants and shrubs along this stretch, where revegetation efforts are under way to undo more than 100 years of sheep and cattle grazing and the proliferation of invasive feed grasses.

A vibrant view from the North Bluff Trail.

At 2.2 miles you'll arrive at the Potato Harbor Overlook (no fence rails so keep young kids close) with its vibrant cove far below in the shape of a potato. There is no coast access from here, so find a nice place to sit and enjoy the view and a picnic if the winds are favorable. Watch for sea lions who sometimes frequent this cove and are easy to spot in the ultra-clear water.

When ready, you'll retrace your steps along the North Bluff Trail, taking care to stay left at the fork (nearest the water) and avoid the dirt service road (Potato Harbor Road)

CAVERN POINT LOOP TO POTATO HARBOR

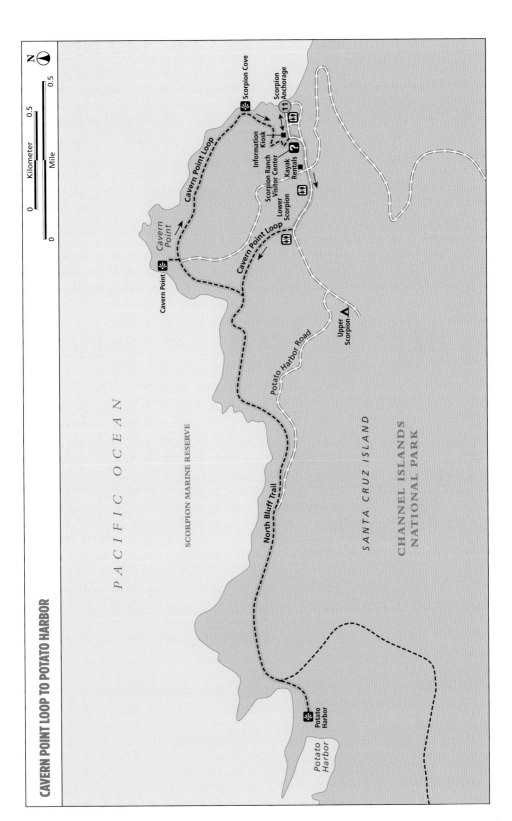

PACIFIC OCEAN

SCORPION MARINE RESERVE

Scorpion Cove

Cavern Point Loop

Cavern Point

Cavern Point

Cavern Point Loop

Information Kiosk

Scorpion Ranch Visitor Center

Lower Scorpion

Scorpion Anchorage

Kayak Rentals

North Bluff Trail

Potato Harbor Road

Upper Scorpion

Potato Harbor

Potato Harbor

SANTA CRUZ ISLAND

CHANNEL ISLANDS NATIONAL PARK

N

Kilometer
0   0.5   0.5

Mile
0   0.5

CAMPING ON SANTA CRUZ?

Want to spend more than a day in Channel Islands National Park? Santa Cruz Island is the easiest for planning a first family island camping trip. The Lower Scorpion Campground is just a short, level, 0.5-mile walk from the dock with 25 family tent campsites, vault toilets, and potable water taps. Just be sure to make your reservation for this popular campground *and* your ferry transportation well in advance! You'll find tips for camping at Scorpion Campground at https://islandpackers.com and www.recreation.gov.

leading back to the campground. At 3.8 miles, you'll intercept Cavern Point Loop and take the left (north) fork to continue the loop in a clockwise direction. As you begin your steepest ascent toward Cavern Point, you'll appreciate that your family only needs to hike up this slope of dirt and loose rocks. Hiking this section in the opposite direction, with the view of the water beyond the staggering cliffs below, has been known to inspire vertigo in some individuals (and palpitations in anyone with kids who may be tempted to take the downhill too quickly).

At 4 miles, you'll reach the Cavern Point Lookout with seating area and, just beyond, the daring spur trail to the Cavern Point Overlook (respect signs if this is closed for any reason on your visit, including unsafe weather conditions). From here your clockwise loop continues along the north side of the island, where you may catch enviable glimpses of anchored yachts and sailboats or brightly colored kayaks below.

At 4.6 miles, you'll reach the Scorpion Cove Overlook with the pier and beach below. Finish your clockwise loop with a rapid descent delivering you near the Scorpion Ranch house. Explore the visitor center and informational displays at your leisure as you make your way back toward the pier and sandy cobblestone beach.

MILES AND DIRECTIONS

0.0 Walk west (straight) from Scorpion Anchorage, passing restrooms and info kiosk.

0.1 Turn left in front of the visitor center (ignore sign to your right for Cavern Point), then right to follow around fenced private property.

0.2 Pass second set of restrooms and continue straight toward campground.

0.4 Go to right (northwest) to pass through the campground toward Cavern Point and Potato Overlook sign.

0.6 Reach the first overlook on Cavern Point Loop, then go left (west) onto North Bluff Trail.

2.2 Arrive at Potato Harbor Overlook; double back on North Bluff Trail, staying left (near water).

3.8 Connect with Cavern Point Loop and stay straight (north) to continue it clockwise.

4.0 Arrive at Cavern Point Lookout; continue clockwise on main trail.

4.6 Arrive at Scorpion Cove Overlook.

5.0 Return to the trailhead (back near dock).

SOUTHERN SIERRA

California's Southern Sierra begins where its famous neighbor to the north, Yosemite National Park, ends—with worthy rivals for majesty as even John Muir himself argued.

In Kings Canyon National Park, you'll find both the highest peak in the contiguous United States, Mt. Whitney at 14,505 feet, as well the more-than-a-mile-deep, glacier-carved Kings Canyon—one of the deepest canyons in North America.

And when it comes to the area's oldest residents, California's world-famous giant sequoias, the superlatives only continue. Here you'll find both the world's largest and second-largest living trees by volume: the General Sherman Tree in Sequoia National Park and the General Grant Tree in Kings Canyon respectively.

With family-friendly hikes through alpine meadows, among giant sequoias, atop granite domes, and alongside crystalline rivers, the Southern Sierra is a magical, must-see region to explore with your child.

South Fork of the Kings River, Kings Canyon National Park.

Following are seven memorable hikes, ranging from easy to moderate/strenuous, to bring these natural wonders of the Southern Sierra to life for your family.

12 BOOLE TREE LOOP

Only 5 miles from bustling General Grant Grove, this quiet trail leads you through mixed pines and manzanita, wildflowers, and beckoning boulders, to the sixth-largest giant sequoia in the world—and by some standards, its sixth-largest tree.

Start: At the signed trailhead at the west end of the parking area
Elevation gain: 570 feet
Distance: 2.5-mile loop
Difficulty: Moderate to strenuous due to rapid elevation gain (starting from an already-high elevation) and steep grades up to 18 percent
Hiking time: About 2 hours
Ages on foot: 5 years+
Seasons/schedule: May through Oct, when the dirt access road is dry
Fees: Free (though you will likely already have a national parks pass for Sequoia-Kings Canyon if you're visiting this area)
Trail contact: Hume Lake Ranger District, 35860 East Kings Canyon Rd., Dunlap 93621, (559) 338-2251, www.fs.usda.gov/recarea/sequoia/
Trail surface: Dirt and rock
Land status: National monument managed by the USDA Forest Service
Nearest town: Squaw Valley
Dogs: Yes, on leash
Toilets: At trailhead
Maps: Map displayed at trailhead, printable map on Forest Service website page for Boole Tree (Converse Basin Grove)
Special considerations: Possible rattlesnakes and bears; heat and altitude can be extra challenging on the steep sections of this trail

FINDING THE TRAILHEAD

This is not a route for low-clearance vehicles, but average sedans generally make the trip in and out taking care with rocks and potholes in the road, and not slowing too much in areas with loose dirt. From Grant Grove Village, drive 4.2 miles east on CA 180 (you will actually be driving north). Ignore navigation that tells you to turn off earlier for the forest roads of the Chicago Stump area. Instead, turn left (also north) onto FR 13S55 where you'll see a sign for "Converse Basin Grove, Stump Meadow, Boole Tree Trail." Continue for 1.9 miles of cautious adventure on this narrowing dirt road, past the aptly named Stump Meadow, where you'll see remnants of the Boole Tree's contemporaries. You'll see the dirt road to/from the Converse Basin Grove joining from the left (west), as you continue straight (north) another 0.8 mile to the parking area with restroom. The signed trailhead with information kiosk is at the west end of the parking area. **GPS:** N36 49.2' / W118 57.6'

THE HIKE

The hike starts at the signed trailhead with a map showing an overview of the Boole Tree Loop. As you pass through the narrow wooden fencing, stay left to make a clockwise loop.

The climb begins immediately, passing through a sparse forest of mixed pines. In spring and summer months, several species of wildflowers brighten the sunny patches you'll pass throughout this hike, including wild rose, penstemon, mariposa lily, and California yellow-eyed grass among others.

At 0.2 mile you'll level off briefly and pass through the first of two gates on this trail (be sure to leave it as you found it). Then it's back to the uphill climb as views northwest toward Kings Canyon gorge begin to emerge through the thin pines to your left (best

Approaching the 2,000-year-old Boole Tree.

in early morning lighting). As the trail steepens to a 14 percent to 18 percent grade, oak trees cast welcome shade and ferns dot the edges of the trail as you near an excellent resting point.

At 0.5 mile you'll find some welcome level ground with an informal side trail leading you out toward a point marked by large, stacked boulders surrounded by deciduous trees. Approach the boulders with care to alert any critters that may be near, and climb up to enjoy a memorable, shady picnic with a view.

Top: Standing at the Base of the Boole Tree beside old fire scars.
Bottom: Pack along a picnic lunch to enjoy in dappled shade atop this rocky overlook.

When ready, pick up the trail and continue around the bend (south), where you'll gain views of Spanish Mountain as you work your way up a series of switchbacks. At 0.8 mile you'll pass through the second gate and find yourself in an area feeling much like a mountaintop, dominated by granite boulders and the burnt trunks of trees.

The Rough Fire blazed through this area in 2015, coming frightfully close to the Boole Tree from multiple directions. The massive wildfire scorched 151,000 acres of

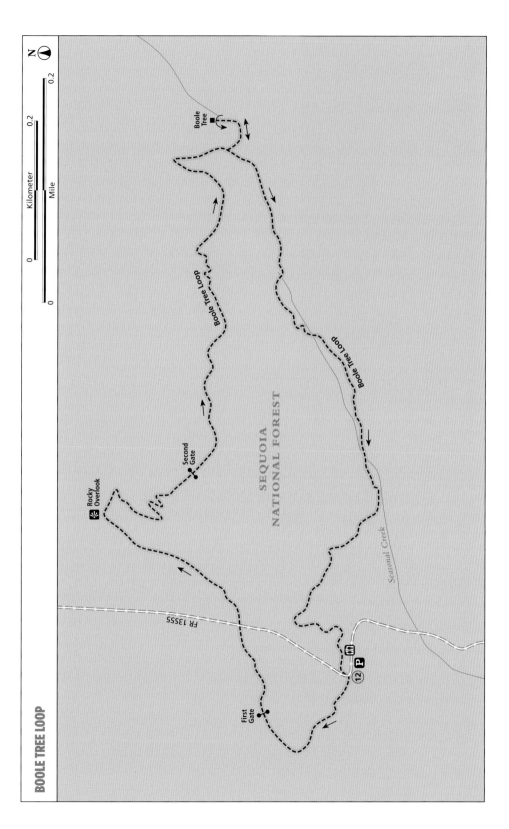

BOOLE TREE LOOP

N

Kilometer
0   0.2

Mile
0   0.2   0.2

Boole Tree

Boole Tree Loop

Boole Tree Loop

SEQUOIA
NATIONAL FOREST

Rocky
Overlook

Second
Gate

First
Gate

FR 13S55

Seasonal Creek

12

P

Pause for a delightful mountain view as you descend toward the Boole Tree spur.

forest and took 99 days to contain—with 3,700 fire personnel assigned to the wildfire at one point.

Now, you can marvel at the stark contrast between the charred snags and survivor trees, and the regenerating forest floor of saplings, shrubbery, and wildflowers.

Soon, the trail takes a hard right (south) and you'll begin a long, straight descent ending at a fork. Continue on the downhill fork to the left (southeast) to visit the Boole Tree. You'll see an informational sign ahead on the left side (north) of this shady spur trail, and when you reach it, you'll see the silent giant standing due north of you, down a secondary trail.

Unlike most of the named giants in the neighboring national parks, you can get up close to the Boole Tree. But with its 35-foot diameter, it's a good challenge to try and hug! Be sure to walk all the way around the base of the tree to fully take in and appreciate its size and age—an estimated 2,000 years.

At 275 feet tall, the Boole Tree is the equivalent of 25 stories. While it looms well above its neighbors today, it was one of a thousand giant sequoias populating the Converse Basin until 1892. In a matter of 25 years, a logging operation decimated these giants, leaving only 60 scattered giants behind—including this one, spared by the logging supervisor for which it is named: Frank Boole.

When ready, backtrack to the main trail and continue your clockwise loop, now heading southwest. After an initial uphill climb including steps, you'll hike down through an area that grows lusher with lupine, wild rose, and grasses as you approach a seasonal streambed. Even when dried to a muddy streak, this zone can be a haven for butterflies, so be sure to slow down and watch for their dazzling wings of orange, lemon yellow, and pale blue.

From here, the trail returns to the parking area, passing behind the restroom and closing the loop back at the trailhead.

MILES AND DIRECTIONS

0.0   Start by leaving the trailhead toward the left.

0.2   Pass through the first gate.

0.5   Reach a rocky overlook.

0.8   Pass through the second gate.

1.4   Take the left fork (southeast) downhill for Boole Tree Spur, then finish loop.

2.5   Return to the trailhead.

13 NORTH GROVE AND DEAD GIANT LOOP

This quiet alternative to Kings Canyon and Sequoia National Parks' busier trails provides the chance to walk through a peaceful High Sierra forest setting with occasional giant sequoia sightings and excellent wildflower viewing in late spring and early summer. The outbound journey ends at an inspiring lookout over Sequoia Lake, the perfect spot to enjoy a family picnic before your return.

Start: At the North Grove sign found at the far west end of the lower General Grant Tree parking area
Elevation gain: 360 feet
Distance: 2.8-mile double loop with spur to overlook
Difficulty: Moderate
Hiking time: 1.5 to 2 hours
Ages on foot: 5 years+
Seasons/schedule: Apr through Oct, but best in spring and early summer when you may catch the dogwoods and wildflowers in bloom
Fees: Weekly vehicle pass $$$$, annual national parks pass, or Every Kid Outdoors Pass (free for fourth graders)
Trail contact: Sequoia and Kings Canyon National Parks, 47050 Generals Hwy., Three Rivers 93271, (559) 565-3341, www.nps.gov/seki; Grant Grove Visitor Center, 3 miles east of the Big Stump entrance station
Trail surface: Dirt and rock
Land status: National park
Nearest town: Squaw Valley

Dogs: No dogs allowed on any trails in Sequoia and Kings Canyon National Parks
Toilets: Flush toilets with diaper changing station at Grant Grove parking area
Water availability: Drinking fountain at restrooms at Grant Grove parking area
Maps: These trails are not clearly labeled on most park maps, but you can search for "North Grove and Dead Giant Loop" in the National Park App and zoom in to see clear labels of trail segments. There is also an overview map posted at the trailhead you can photograph. However, the more detailed "Grant Grove Trail Map" of this area, which includes these and other clearly labeled nearby trails, is available for purchase at the Grant Grove Visitor Center.
Other trail users: Equestrians
Special considerations: Possible poison oak near trail and biting insects in meadow areas; bring insect repellent in case

FINDING THE TRAILHEAD

From Kings Canyon Visitor Center, drive north on CA 180 for 0.2 mile, then turn left (west) onto Grant Tree Road. In 0.8 mile you'll turn right (north) into the primary parking area for the General Grant Grove, where you'll see the Grant Tree Trail begin. Continue west toward the lower parking area, reserved for RVs and trailers. You'll find the sign for the "North Grove Trails" at the west end of this parking area. **GPS:** N36 44.50' / W118 50.30'

THE HIKE

Begin at the signed trailhead for "North Grove Trails," taking a photo of the informational map for reference if you don't have an alternative map with you (don't rely on

Exploring a path less traveled: North Grove Trail in Kings Canyon National Park.

steady GPS in this section of the park). Walk around the gate crossing this fire road, which is also the first section of the Sunset Trail you'll hike on this journey.

Proceed along the wide path through the shade of towering cedars and pines until the trail forks at 0.1 mile, where you'll take the right (west / northwest) as the sign instructs to follow the North Grove Trail (the Sunset Trail / fire road continues on the left side, which you'll take on your return).

From here your path narrows slightly, losing the fire-road feeling as greenery and wildflower foliage close in. Suddenly the first giant sequoia of the route looms ahead of you.

Continue following the trail as it winds around meadow patches with occasional giants standing guard on this peaceful path less traveled. Soon, you'll find yourself in a lush understory of Pacific dogwood, which you may be lucky enough to catch in bloom in early summer.

As the trail begins to climb, you'll pass into a section of fire-scarred forest, where the Rough Fire of 2015 blazed as firefighters worked heroically to protect the ancient giants of the area, including those in the nearby Grant Grove itself, which were thankfully spared. Today, you'll see life springing back through this section, with young trees already taking root alongside California lilac, wild iris, and wild strawberry.

At 1.3 miles you'll arrive at the second junction with the Sunset Trail and turn right (southwest) onto the wide fire road. As lush Lion Meadow comes into view

Pacific dogwood and ferns close in on a magical stretch of the North Grove Trail.

on your right (west), look for the massive sequoia lying across the meadow, spanning from one side to the other. This fallen soldier, however, is *not* the Dead Giant.

At 1.5 miles you'll see the small sign for the Dead Giant Loop to your right (northwest), with both ends of the trail visible. When hiking with kids, I recommend taking the left side first as it's more direct to your picnic destination and saves the Dead Giant for your return.

When you reach the top of the trail (1.7 miles), don't be surprised that your view, though lovely, shows no sign of water. You'll take the less noticeable, unmarked spur to your left (south) until Sequoia Lake comes into view in the distance. Perch yourselves on the boulders here and enjoy a picnic with a view.

When ready, return to the Dead Giant Loop trail and continue straight (north) where you left off. As the trail curves toward your right (southeast), behold the fire-scarred, moss-clad Dead Giant itself: a massive, eerie, expired sequoia that—thus far—refuses to fall.

Top: Young trees and foliage emerge among the fire-scarred giant sequoias surviving the Rough Fire in Kings Canyon National Park.
Bottom: The Sequoia Lake Overlook at the top of Dead Giant Loop is a prime spot for a family picnic.

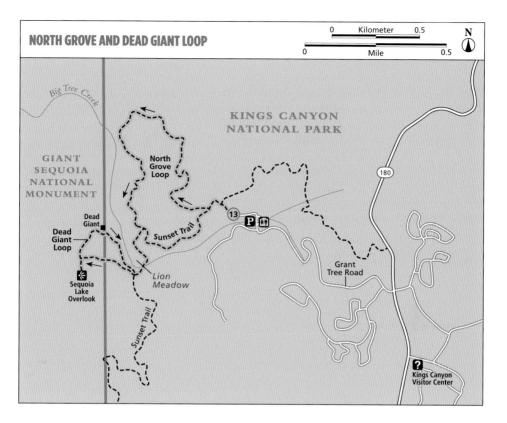

NORTH GROVE AND DEAD GIANT LOOP

0   Kilometer   0.5

0   Mile   0.5

N

Big Tree Creek

KINGS CANYON
NATIONAL PARK

GIANT
SEQUOIA
NATIONAL
MONUMENT

North
Grove
Loop

180

Dead
Giant

Dead
Giant
Loop

Sunset Trail

13

P

Lion
Meadow

Grant
Tree Road

Sequoia
Lake
Overlook

Sunset Trail

Sunset Trail

Kings Canyon
Visitor Center

Continue along the loop with views of Lion Meadow to your left. At 2 miles you'll return to the junction of Dead Giant Loop and the Sunset Trail. Turn left (northeast) to retrace your steps 0.2 mile back toward the North Grove junction.

Here you'll take the right (south) to continue on the Sunset Trail, then stay right again (southeast) at the North Grove Trail junction to return back to the trailhead.

MILES AND DIRECTIONS

0.0   Start at the signed trailhead.

0.1   Take the right (northwest) path at North Grove Loop Junction.

1.3   Turn right onto Sunset Trail.

1.5   Go right (northwest) at the start of Dead Giant Loop trail, taking the left fork of the loop.

1.7   Turn left (south) on the spur trail to Sequoia Lake overlook.

1.9   Take in the view of the Dead Giant.

2.0   Return to Sunset Trail junction and go left (northeast).

2.2   Arrive at the junction with North Grove Loop; go right (south) onto Sunset Trail.

2.5   Stay to the right (southeast) to remain on Sunset Trail.

2.8   Arrive back at the trailhead.

14 GENERAL GRANT LOOP

As the second-largest tree in the world by volume, the General Grant Tree itself is worth a visit to the Grant Grove. But this living national shrine, whose base could span three lanes of a freeway, is just one of the many attractions along this stroller-friendly, 0.5-mile historic trail. The General Grant Loop is also located in the most easily accessed part of Kings Canyon National Park, close to campgrounds, lodging, and dining, which makes it a great introduction to Sequoia National Park's less-visited but no-less-beautiful neighbor to the north.

Start: Trailhead for the General Grant Grove at east end of parking area
Elevation gain: 26 feet
Distance: 0.5-mile loop with additional offshoot trails to explore
Difficulty: Easy
Hiking time: 30 minutes to 1 hour
Ages on foot: 3 years+
Seasons/schedule: Late Apr through Oct, though winter visits may be possible depending on conditions (ask about snowshoe rentals at the Grant Grove Gift Shop)
Fees: Weekly vehicle pass $$$$, annual national parks pass, or Every Kid Outdoors Pass (free for fourth graders)
Trail contact: Sequoia and Kings Canyon National Parks, 47050 Generals Hwy., Three Rivers 93271, (559) 565-3341, www.nps.gov/seki; Grant Grove Visitor Center, 3 miles east of the Big Stump entrance station

Trail surface: Paved, with additional dirt trails
Land status: National park
Nearest town: Squaw Valley
Dogs: No dogs allowed on any trails in Sequoia and Kings Canyon National Parks
Toilets: Flush toilets with diaper changing station in parking area
Maps: Downloadable trail map at www.visitsequoia.com and on the National Park App. A more detailed "Grant Grove Trail Map," which includes other nearby trails, is available for purchase at the Grant Grove Visitor Center, but for the best information about the trees in the grove, purchase the interpretive General Grant Tree Trail pamphlet with map from the Sequoia Parks Conservancy available at the trailhead.

FINDING THE TRAILHEAD

 From Kings Canyon Visitor Center, drive north on CA 180 for 0.2 mile, then turn left (west) onto Grant Tree Road. In 0.8 mile you'll turn right (north) into the primary car parking area for General Grant Grove, where you'll see the well-marked "Grant Tree Trail" begin. **GPS:** N36 44.50' / W118 58.25'

THE HIKE

Start at the "Grant Tree Trail" informational sign on the north side of the main parking area (opposite the restrooms), and proceed to your right (east) up the paved trail. You'll quickly arrive at the second-largest tree in this grove and one of the fifteen largest trees on earth: the Robert E. Lee Tree. And just behind it, you'll discover what will be for many kids the most memorable part of this trail: the Fallen Monarch.

If walls could talk, the interior of this storied sequoia would not disappoint. After a fierce hollowing out by fire, the tree fell some 300 years ago. Since then, known

Visitors pass by the mighty Lincoln tree with its 21-foot diameter base.

inhabitants of the Fallen Monarch have included the Gamlin brothers while they built the cabin you'll visit farther along this trail, the gentlemen responsible for cutting down the tree now marked by the Centennial Stump, and some thirty-two horses belonging to the US Cavalry. For a brief time, the Fallen Monarch also served as a hotel and saloon. Take a stroll inside the tree before continuing up the trail where you left off. (You'll have another chance to visit it on the other side of the loop.)

Top: Take a stroll inside the Fallen Monarch to see if you can find evidence of its past lives as saloon and horse stable.
Bottom: Step inside the historic Gamlin Cabin as you learn more about the early efforts to log—and then save these giants.

Next, watch for a "photo point" sign on your left. It won't be obvious until you pause directly in front of the sign that you have a majestic view of the General Grant Tree through a forest of younger trees. This near top-to-bottom view of the 286-foot giant, in contrast with the "junior sequoias," will surely help you appreciate its estimated 1,700 years on earth.

Continue following the main, paved path in a counterclockwise direction until you find the sign "To see Grant Tree fire scar" with stone steps leading up to your right (north). Venture up this path to get a good look at General Grant's fire-marred backside. While it's not the most uplifting sight, the 2-story-high burn mark is a good reminder of how much these giants can—and have—endured.

Follow the fire-scar path around General Grant to where it rejoins the paved loop trail to your left (west) and take in the more photogenic view of the General. In 0.2 mile take the right (north) toward the Gamlin Cabin. Built in 1872, the cabin first housed enterprising brothers Israel and Thomas Gamlin who had filed a timber claim to 160 acres within Grant Grove and also grazed cattle nearby. Thankfully, in 1880, the US surveyor general for California withdrew four sections of land for sale surrounding the General Grant Tree.

And in 1890, thanks to naturalist John Muir's efforts to help bring attention to the treasures of this region, Congress passed the bill establishing Yosemite, Sequoia, and General Grant National Parks (the latter would be absorbed into Kings Canyon National Park in 1940). The giants of Grant Grove were officially protected, and (somewhat poetically) the Gamlin Cabin would come to house the first park ranger stationed here.

After visiting the cabin, continue counterclockwise (southwest) on the paved trail as it starts down the west side of the loop, where more mighty giants await. But first, take a moment to pay your respects to the Centennial Stump on your left—all that remains of a 24-foot diameter sequoia chopped down in 1875 so that 16 feet of its mighty trunk could be displayed at the Philadelphia Centennial Exhibit. Sadly, since the tree's trunk was sent in sections to be reassembled, visitors to the exhibit didn't believe it had ever been a single tree and dubbed it "The California Hoax."

As you near completion of the loop, you'll pass by the base of the Fallen Monarch with one last chance to step inside. On the final sloping stretch of this trail, slow down to get a good look at the magnificent Lincoln Tree on your left (east) with its 21-foot diameter measured at chest height.

Once you've returned to the trailhead, you may wish to take a closer look at the parking lot's celebrity Twin Sisters, the unmistakable conjoined giant sequoias at the west end, and the photogenic Happy Family group of giants at the southeast end near the restrooms. But for a fun surprise, take your family to the short Michigan Tree Trail,

O, CHRISTMAS TREE!

In April of 1926, President Calvin Coolidge designated the General Grant Tree as the Nation's Christmas Tree. Since then, residents of nearby Sanger (recognized by the US Post Office as "The Nation's Christmas Tree City") and visitors make an annual trek to pay tribute to the tree and celebrate the season in the spirit of "peace on earth and good will to all." The official gathering, which takes place the second Sunday of every December, has only been interrupted during war years when travel was restricted due to gas rationing, and in 2020 due to the Covid-19 pandemic. But even in those difficult years, a member of the National Park Service kept the tradition alive by visiting the tree and placing a holiday wreath ceremonially at its base.

The Rivoli kids stand with the Twin Sisters of General Grant Grove, a fused pair of giant sequoias.

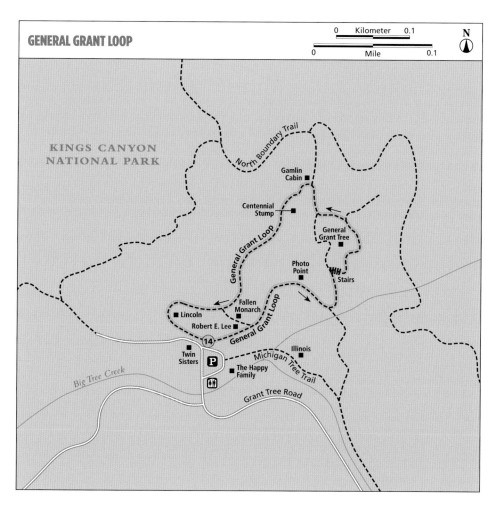

which begins between the Happy Family and General Grant Loop trailhead. Look for the awesome Illinois tree just a short way in on your left (north), where you'll be able to stand in the fire-scarred mouth of the giant's trunk—and your kids may be able to climb through its cavernous base and come out the other side.

MILES AND DIRECTIONS

0.0   Start at trailhead and bear right (west) toward Robert E. Lee and Fallen Monarch trees.

0.1   Arrive at Photo Point, continue following main, paved path.

0.2   Take stairs to your right (north). Ignore spur trail and continue straight on paved path.

0.3   Take right up toward Gamlin Cabin; continue southwest on main path.

0.4   Arrive at opposite end of Fallen Monarch.

0.5   Finish loop and arrive back at trailhead.

15 ZUMWALT MEADOW TO MUIR ROCK

Hike along the pristine South Fork of the Kings River with views of verdant Zumwalt Meadow and spectacular granite faces along your way. After clambering up and over—and even under—some massive granite boulders, you'll pass through an otherworldly forest of contrasts with blackened tree trunks from recent prescriptive burns and new, bright green growth springing up from the earth as the forest floor regenerates. As you pass through the final, shady forest stretch, you'll arrive at historic Muir Rock, jutting out above the river and crying out for your picnic lunch.

Start: Trailhead at Zumwalt Meadow parking area
Elevation gain: 226 feet
Distance: 3.2-mile out-and-back
Difficulty: Moderate because of multiple sections with steep steps up and down through granite and traversing some loose granite rocks
Hiking time: About 2 hours
Ages on foot: 5 years+
Seasons/schedule: Late spring to early Oct. Kings Canyon Scenic Byway (this section of SR 180) closes for the winter so be sure to check current conditions if visiting at either end of this timeframe
Fees: Weekly vehicle pass $$$$, annual national parks pass, or Every Kid Outdoors Pass (*free* for fourth graders and their families)
Trail contact: Sequoia & Kings Canyon National Parks, 47050 Generals Hwy., Three Rivers 93271, (559) 565-3341, www.nps.gov/seki; Cedar Grove Visitor Center, 29 miles from Grant Grove on CA 180
Trail surface: Dirt, stone, and chunks of granite gravel
Land status: National park
Nearest town: Squaw Valley

Dogs: No dogs allowed on any trails in Sequoia and Kings Canyon National Parks
Toilets: Vault toilets at Zumwalt Meadow Trailhead and at Road's End staging area
Maps: National Parks App or see the digital Sequoia and Kings Canyon Park Atlas in the Day Hikes section of www.NPS.gov/seki. A detailed map is also posted at the trailhead information kiosks.
Other trail users: Backpackers
Special considerations: The river can be beautiful while still swift and hazardous. The beach beside Muir Rock is a popular swimming area when the water gets low enough (and many daredevils also jump from Muir Rock)—but many visitors have made the mistake of assuming this water is safe when it isn't. Don't take any chances, especially with kids who might not be able to regain their footing if they slip into a swift current even in shallow water, and check with the rangers about the latest conditions before getting into the water here.

FINDING THE TRAILHEAD

From the Kings Canyon Visitor Center at Grant Grove Village, you'll drive 33.4 miles east on Kings Canyon Scenic Byway (CA 180 E), a spectacular drive of diminishing elevation that takes approximately 1 hour (road closed in winter). At the sign for Zumwalt Meadow, turn right (southeast) into the parking area. The Zumwalt Meadow / Roaring River Trailhead is at the south end of the parking area.
GPS: N36 47.62' / W118 35.91'

The Rivoli family (minus photographer) enjoys a riverside picnic lunch atop Muir Rock.

THE HIKE

The hike begins on the north side of the South Fork of the Kings River with lovely glimpses of the water between pine trees and the towering granite Grand Sentinel on the opposite side. Watch for the "saguaro cedar" in the middle of the path—a large, cactus-shaped incense cedar often mistaken for a sequoia because of its wide, reddish trunk and absence of lower branches, which were lost to fire years ago—an adaptation that has helped it survive fires since.

The spectacular South Fork of the Kings River is a treasure of the Sierras.

As the trail narrows and forest closes in, you'll come upon a wooden suspension bridge leading you to the south side of the river, where you'll take a left (east) onto the Zumwalt Meadow / River Trail. Zumwalt Meadow was once a loop trail, until flooding took out the northern boardwalk section in 2019 and altered the course of the river. You may still see it referenced as a loop on other trail maps, guides, and even some trail signs, but it's now used as an out-and-back trail (please respect the trail closure signs) and as a connector trail.

Enjoy the shady, easy walk along here, as the trees begin to open up with views of lush Zumwalt Meadow and North Dome towering above. An informal path leads toward the meadow's edge if you'd like to step out for a better view and check for wildlife.

Continuing east, you will follow the trail onto your first section of granite boulders and gravel to traverse. Soon after, you'll encounter more challenging boulders to traverse up and down, and up and down again with occasional views over Zumwalt Meadow and its patches of evergreens (this is the elevation gain section of the otherwise fairly flat hike). If you have a lizard enthusiast in your family, this area has additional benefits.

At 0.8 mile the Zumwalt Meadow Trail ends, and you'll take the right fork (east) to continue on the River Trail following the sign toward Road's End. From here, you'll journey through a section of forest that underwent a prescription burn (planned fire) in recent years, where fire-scarred mature trees are surrounded by the bright green growth of young trees and shrubbery.

Eventually, the trail leads you back to the river where you'll hike with tree-framed views of this fly-fishing paradise until coming upon another set of large granite boulders. This time, you'll follow the path beneath them in a short, natural tunnel.

As you arrive back at the river, cross the wide Red Bridge back to the north side. Continue on the River Trail until you arrive at the information kiosk for the River Trail at the edge of the Road's End parking area. From here, you can take the shortcut trail (about seven parking spaces in) toward your right (south) and to Muir Rock. Or continue

Enjoy a shady water break with a view of Zumwalt Meadow.

ZUMWALT MEADOW TO MUIR ROCK

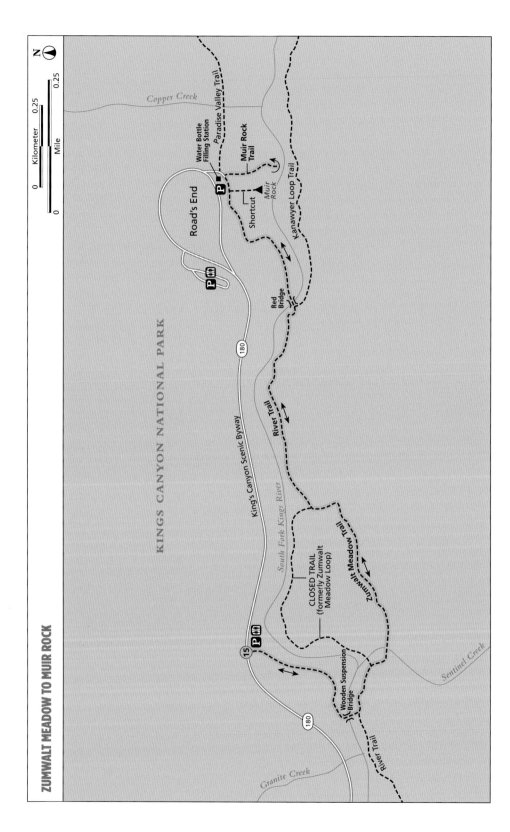

KINGS CANYON NATIONAL PARK

Copper Creek

Road's End

Water Bottle
Filling Station

Paradise Valley Trail

Muir Rock
Trail

Shortcut

Muir
Rock

Kanawyer Loop Trail

Red
Bridge

King's Canyon Scenic Byway

River Trail

South Fork Kings River

CLOSED TRAIL
(formerly Zumwalt
Meadow Loop)

Zumwalt Meadow Trail

Sentinel Creek

Wooden Suspension
Bridge

Granite Creek

River Trail

N

Kilometer   0.25

Mile   0.25

on to use the restrooms at this parking area and top off your water bottles before taking the trail farther along the parking area toward the river and Muir Rock, where the large, flat landmark juts into the water.

Find the natural step up and walk carefully out to enjoy your "Muir Rock Moment," standing above the glorious green-blue water on the very spot where famed naturalist John Muir spoke to small groups more than 100 years ago, sharing his theories of how Kings Canyon and others like it were formed and his love and appreciation of its unspoiled wilderness. Muir's talks and writings about Kings Canyon played a critical role in the eventual creation of this national park and protection of this land.

When ready, double back along the same trails to where you began.

MILES AND DIRECTIONS

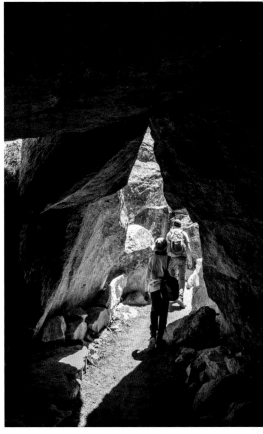

Venturing beneath big granite boulders along the River Trail portion of the hike.

0.0	Head south from the parking lot on Zumwalt Meadow / Roaring River Falls Trail.
0.2	Cross the wooden suspension bridge.
0.3	Turn left (east) onto the River Trail.
0.4	Take right fork (southeast) onto Zumwalt Meadow Trail (left fork closed).
0.8	Turn right (east) onto River Trail.
1.2	Take a left (north) and cross the Red Bridge.
1.4	Arrive at River Trail sign at edge of Road's End parking area. Either take the shortcut trail to your right (south) to the river or continue straight through the parking area to the water filling station.
1.5	At east edge of parking lot, top off water bottles, then take Muir Rock Trail south to the river and a slight right (west) along the river to Muir Rock.
1.6	Arrive at Muir Rock. Double back when ready.
3.2	Arrive back at trailhead.

16 LITTLE BALDY

Hike to the summit of this granite dome at 8,044 feet, where you'll enjoy 360-degree views toward the Silliman Crest, Kaweah Peaks, the Great Western Divide, and the San Joaquin Valley.

Start: Signed trailhead on Generals Highway across street from Little Baldy Saddle sign
Elevation gain: 790 feet
Distance: 3.6-mile out-and-back
Difficulty: Moderate to strenuous because of high start elevation and continuous elevation gain (equivalent of a 73-story building) the whole way up. Go slowly and watch for marmots and wildflowers along the way.
Hiking time: 2.5 to 3 hours
Ages on foot: 5 years+ (requires serious stamina for the almost nonstop elevation gain to the top)
Seasons/schedule: Best in summer and early fall. Icy conditions and deep snow may be present in winter and into spring, making portions of the trail and dome unsafe.
Fees: Weekly vehicle pass $$$$, annual national parks pass, or Every Kid Outdoors Pass (free for fourth graders)
Trail contact: Sequoia and Kings Canyon National Parks, 47050 Generals Hwy., Three Rivers 93271,

(559) 565-3341, www.nps.gov/seki; Lodgepole Visitor Center, 21 miles north of the Ash Mountain entrance station
Trail surface: Dirt, rocks, and granite face
Land status: National park
Nearest town: Three Rivers
Dogs: No dogs allowed on any trails in Sequoia and Kings Canyon National Parks
Toilets: None at trailhead, but you'll find restrooms about 0.25 mile north on Generals Highway
Maps: USGS Giant Forest and on sign at trailhead
Special considerations: The granite dome of Little Baldy summit is generally a safe place to explore in dry, summer months, but keep kids away from the outermost edges where loose gravel can be present. Lightning strikes are a real risk on Little Baldy, so postpone this hike if you see ominous clouds, sense static electricity in the air, or know of any chance of a storm rolling in.

FINDING THE TRAILHEAD

From Lodgepole, drive 6.6 miles north on Generals Highway, or drive 1.5 miles south from Dorst Campground. Watch for the "Little Baldy Saddle" sign on the west side of the highway, with spaces for roadside parking along each side. You'll find the signed trailhead for "Little Baldy Trail" with four wide steps leading the way on the east side of the highway (north end of the roadside parking). **GPS:** N36 37.2' / W118 48'

THE HIKE

Pack your lunches and lace up your shoes for one of the most memorable picnic spots included in this guide. The hike starts at the Little Baldy Saddle section of Generals Highway, at an already respectable 7,335 feet above sea level.

If you've just arrived from a significantly lower elevation, be especially sure to pace yourselves as you begin the climb with short, shady switchbacks followed by long, steadily building switchbacks for the first two–thirds up the mountain.

Descending Little Baldy summit with a view of Mt. Silliman to the east.

In early summer you'll have plenty of occasions to stop and catch your breath while admiring the diverse wildflowers you're likely find along this route. Despite the severe fire scarring on this slope from the 2021 KNP Complex Fire, you might spy penstemon, Wright's blue-eyed Mary, whiskerbrush, and lavender lupine among others.

At only 0.4 mile into the hike, your climbing efforts are rewarded by views of Big Baldy and Chimney Rock to the west. And for those who tread lightly and keep a keen eye out, this next portion of the trail also offers excellent marmot-viewing opportunities. Watch for them posing stoically among the boulders and logs along the way.

Top: The first view of the Kaweahs opens up to the east.
Bottom: A picnic to remember: Lunch on the summit of Little Baldy.

Around 1 mile the trail levels off briefly, leading you through a more exposed area of charred tree trunks and granite boulders, where low-growing greenery already rebounds along the trail sides.

At 1.5 miles your view to the east begins to open up above the treetops. Watch for the large expanse of granite to your right (east) where the trail subtly forks. Rather than continue straight on the flat dirt path alongside the granite, follow along the faintly worn path up to your right (southwest) onto the top of this rock face for a marvelous first view of the Kaweahs and Great Western Divide (and a great spot to rest and rehydrate).

From here just continue south along the rocky surface until you rejoin the dirt trail (which runs pretty much parallel below). Enjoy a last bit of shade and level land before

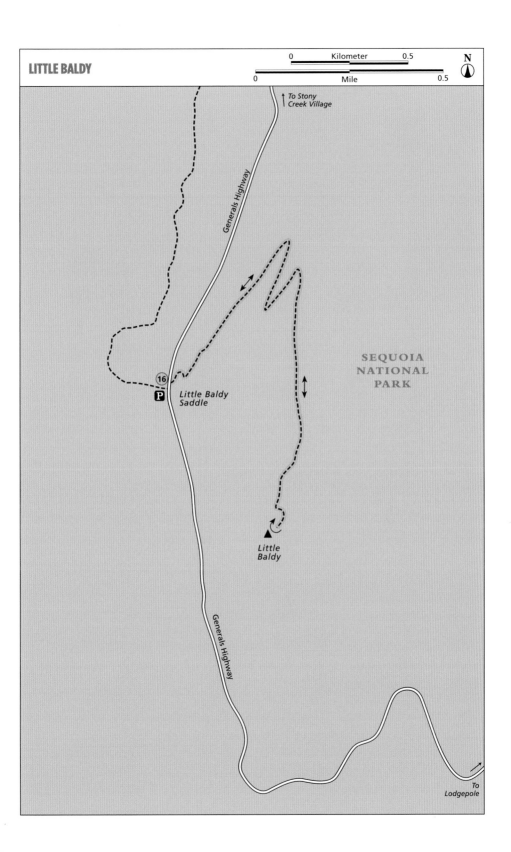

LITTLE BALDY

0 Kilometer 0.5

0 Mile 0.5

N

To Stony
Creek Village

Generals Highway

SEQUOIA
NATIONAL
PARK

16

P

Little Baldy
Saddle

Little
Baldy

Generals Highway

To
Lodgepole

CUTE (BUT CRAFTY) CRITTERS

Marmots are the largest members of the squirrel family, growing as big as some very well-fed house cats. While they are generally a delight to observe in the wild, marmots in the Mineral King area of Sequoia National Park have developed a pesky pastime of chewing radiator hoses and sometimes causing other damage to visitors' vehicles. If visiting that part of the park, be sure to follow the NPS guidance for protecting your vehicle (and the marmots)! www.NPS.gov/SEKI

A yellow-bellied marmot sighting on the hike up Little Baldy.

large stony steps begin leading you up yet higher and toward the peak. At the tree line look for the first in a series of informal rock cairns, which will lead you on your best route up the granite dome, curving around the left side (from the south) and on up to the top until you find yourselves standing at the US Geological Survey marker at the summit of Little Baldy: 8,044 feet above sea level.

Take in the 360-degree view over Sequoia National Park, with Spanish Mountain and Obelisk to the north. Mount Silliman, Alta Peak, the Kaweahs, and Great Western Divide stand majestically to the east. And to the west, you'll see Big Baldy and, if it's clear, the San Joaquin Valley stretching into the distance.

Even on a busy summer weekend, you're unlikely to encounter a crowd up here. So take a seat and pull out those sandwiches, which you may find more astonishingly delicious than expected. Everything tastes better when you're sitting on top of the world.

MILES AND DIRECTIONS

0.0   Start at the trailhead.

0.4   Enjoy a view of Big Baldy and Chimney Rock.

1.5   Take a slight right (southwest) up onto the granite face; continue parallel to the trail.

1.8   Attain the summit of Little Baldy; reverse course when ready.

3.6   Arrive back at the trailhead.

17 **TOKOPAH FALLS**

Hike alongside the pristine Marble Fork of the Kaweah River as it splashes and spills over one set of boulders after the next. In case the scenery along the way isn't pretty enough, your continual climb is ultimately rewarded with a view of 1,200-foot Tokopah Falls, the tallest waterfall in Sequoia National Park.

Start: At the signed trailhead left of Log Bridge in Lodgepole Campground
Elevation gain: 623 feet
Distance: 3.8-mile out-and-back
Difficulty: Moderate with strenuous portions. (**Note:** This trail is often mislabeled as easy, but it requires stamina—and a snack break—for the steady elevation gain of roughly 57 stories to the falls, starting at a respectable 6,700 feet above sea level.)
Hiking time: 2 to 3 hours
Ages on foot: 7 years+ or Energizer bunnies from 4 years+
Seasons/schedule: Best in spring and early summer when the falls are at their best
Fees: Weekly vehicle pass $$$$, annual national parks pass, or Every Kid Outdoors Pass (free for fourth graders)
Trail contact: Sequoia and Kings Canyon National Parks, 47050

Generals Hwy., Three Rivers 93271, (559) 565-3341, www.nps.gov/seki; Lodgepole Visitor Center, 21 miles north of the Ash Mountain entrance station
Trail surface: Dirt and rock
Land status: National park
Nearest town: Three Rivers
Dogs: No dogs allowed on any trails in Sequoia and Kings Canyon National Parks
Toilets: At parking area
Maps: This trail is shown on the visitor's map provided at park entrances. Additionally, a Tokopah Falls Trail map is included in the National Park App and posted at the trailhead where you can snap a photo with your phone.
Special considerations: The river, though beautiful, can be swift and deadly when full in spring and early summer. Make sure kids know to stay back and on established trails.

FINDING THE TRAILHEAD

From Generals Highway (CA 198), turn east onto Lodgepole Road toward the Lodgepole Visitor Center. Continue east for 0.7 mile (about 2 minutes) on Lodgepole Road and look for parking at the camping overflow parking area near the abandoned Nature Center building. Walk east through the parking area, past the shuttle stop and restrooms, and follow the road sign toward Log Bridge Campsites to your left (northeast), crossing over the bridge. The signed Tokopah Trailhead and information sign are on your right (east) just past the bridge. **GPS:** N36 36.29' / W118 43.49'

THE HIKE

The hike begins on the north end of the rustic stonework and log bridge entrance to the Log Bridge Campsites and follows along the north side of the Marble Fork of the scenic and wildly changeable Kaweah River. In early snowmelt season its water rages through the Tokopah Valley, but it gradually tames to a series of mini waterfalls and pools as summer progresses.

The lower section of 1,200-foot Tokopah Falls.

TOKOPAH FALLS

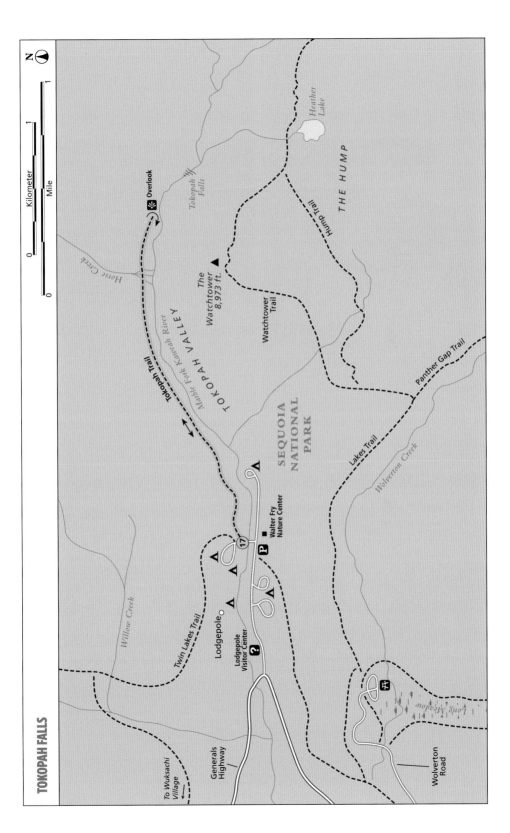

Top left: Hiking to Tokopah Falls with a view of the iconic Watchtower dome.
Top right: Enjoy the shade of lodgepole pines and red fir trees on the first leg of this hike.
Bottom: Passing beneath this massive granite overhang adds an exciting dimension to the hike.

While many side trails will tempt you to get closer to the water, exercise extreme caution and keep your distance (especially with curious children) if there's much water flow at all during your visit. And remember the granite rocks along the river can be extra slippery where wet and/or worn. But not to worry, there are plenty of good views of the river from the proper trail along the way!

The trail begins as a flat, dirt-and-packed-sand path, convincing many the trail is as often incorrectly advertised: easy. But it soon takes on a series of wide-set stone steps as your climb begins. The stone steps become more frequent and closer together as you find yourself moving farther from the river, but in the more consistent shade of lodgepole pines and red fir trees.

Watch as the trailside boulders begin increasing in size—a sign you're making progress toward the waterfall. At 1.4 miles, you'll cross the first of three small footbridges that traverse Horse Creek, a multiforked creek that also changes dramatically from spring through summer months. After crossing your final bridge, the trail soon opens up onto a stunning landscape of glacier-carved canyon walls, with the iconic Watchtower's pointed granite dome looming above it all.

This is where the hike begins passing between, over—and even *beneath* (watch your head!) massive boulders and granite ledges. Watch for curious marmots along this stretch, along with vibrant wildflowers and the butterflies drawn to them.

Suddenly Tokopah Falls appears in the distance, roughly 85 stories of multiple, flowing cascades down the steeply sloping rock face. Pause to enjoy the waterfall in its entirety from here as you won't be able to see all of it once you get up close. Then continue to the Tokopah Falls Overlook and end point for this trail.

If it's too hot (or crowded) to linger over your lunch at the base of the falls, turn back when ready to look for some shady boulders or a log for your picnic on your return journey—which will be much easier and faster as you make your descent back to the trailhead.

MILES AND DIRECTIONS

0.0   Head east from the official Start/End at the Tokopah Falls Trailhead.

1.4   Cross first of three footbridges over Horse Creek.

1.9   Arrive at Tokopah Falls Overlook. When ready, reverse course.

3.8   Return to the trailhead.

18 **MORO ROCK**

At only 0.5 mile round-trip, some might hesitate to call it a hike—until they see the 300-foot elevation gain to be achieved in the first half of that. Conquering "the rock" gives kids a thrill and tremendous sense of accomplishment, and the 360-degree views from the top of Moro Rock aren't bad either. Just be sure kids know to respect the guard-rails, and check anyone's fear of heights at the trailhead!

Start: Moro Rock Trailhead
Elevation gain: 300 feet
Distance: 0.5-mile out-and-back
(**Note:** You can start at the marked Moro Rock Trail at the Giant Forest Museum to add 1.5 miles of not particularly exciting hiking, but with kids in particular, I recommend starting and finishing this challenging hike at the rock.)
Difficulty: Moderate to strenuous
Hiking time: 45 minutes to 1 hour
Ages on foot: 5 years+ (or more cautious, younger Energizer bunnies)
Seasons/schedule: May through early Oct (road closes for snow; trail is unsafe in wet or icy conditions and certainly in lightning)
Fees and permits: $$$$ weekly vehicle pass, annual national parks pass, or Every Kid Outdoors Pass (*free* for fourth graders and their families)

Trail contact: Sequoia and Kings Canyon National Parks, 47050 Generals Hwy., Three Rivers 93271, (559) 565-3341, www.nps.gov/seki; Lodgepole Visitor Center, 21 miles north of the Ash Mountain entrance station
Trail surface: Concrete and stone
Land status: National park
Nearest town: Three Rivers
Dogs: No dogs allowed on any trails in Sequoia and Kings Canyon National Parks
Toilets: At trailhead
Maps: No maps necessary, this hike is one clearly defined route with no intercepting trails
Special considerations: With 1,000-foot drop-offs from the trail, kids need to know to respect the guardrails and not climb on them. Those with vertigo or a fear of heights will want to avoid this hike.

FINDING THE TRAILHEAD

If traveling south from the Lodgepole Visitor Center, take Generals Highway 4.3 miles south to Crescent Meadow Road. If driving north from the Foothills Visitor Center near the south entrance, take Generals Highway north 15.5 miles. Turn south/southeast onto Crescent Meadow Road (just south of the Giant Forest Museum), and at 1.2 miles stay right, then right again as the road becomes a one-way loop (aka Moro Rock Loop). In 0.4 mile you'll arrive at the Moro Rock parking area and the signed trailhead on the south side at the base of the monolith. **GPS:** N36 32.81' / W118 45.94'

THE HIKE

The hike begins with a respectable section of concrete stairs separated by brief landings between trees as you make your way up the left side of Moro Rock. Pace yourselves here—you've got more than 350 steps to climb, in addition to some sloping, inclined sections of trail. Unless you're visiting from Denver or you've already had some days to adjust to the altitude, this hike to 6,725 feet above sea level will likely challenge your lungs as well as your legs (fortunately, you're only hiking the last 300 feet of that).

The Rivoli family at the top of Moro Rock on their first visit as a family of five.

Once you complete this first section of stairs, you'll have a better view of what lies ahead as the path begins to snake through a series of cut-rock slopes and concrete steps up the stunning monolith before you. Most of the trail you see today was created by the Civilian Conservation Corps in 1931 to replace the severely weathered and worn, original wooden staircase built in 1917. Take a moment to catch your breath along here and enjoy the views opening up to the left (east) side of the trail, above the forest canopy.

As you continue, you'll work your way up and over to the west side of Moro Rock, with brief views from both sides as you climb a narrow staircase. Take the turnout to your right to enjoy the first sweeping view of the west side extending through the Middle Fork Canyon of the Kaweah River all the way toward the San Joaquin Valley. An informational sign helps explain how important the great many miles of forest you see before you, nearly all of it the Kaweah Watershed, are to the distant valley and one of California's most productive agricultural regions.

On clear days, from this magnificent vista, you'll be able to see all the way to Triple Divide Peak of the Western Divide. Pause at the informational sign to help identify some of the tallest peaks along the Divide and some of the closer landmarks in Sequoia National Park.

When ready, continue up the final, thrilling sections of stairs, passing narrowly between rocks, until you finally arrive at the unmistakable top of Moro Rock. Go ahead and grab onto the guardrails (and your kids) as you get your bearings. Beyond the relatively level summit is 1,000 feet of vertical drop.

April through mid-August, you may spot peregrine falcons soaring to and from their nesting sites on the west side of Moro Rock. And in the slivers of spring and fall outside of their nesting season, this side becomes a thrilling playground for some of the world's best rock climbers.

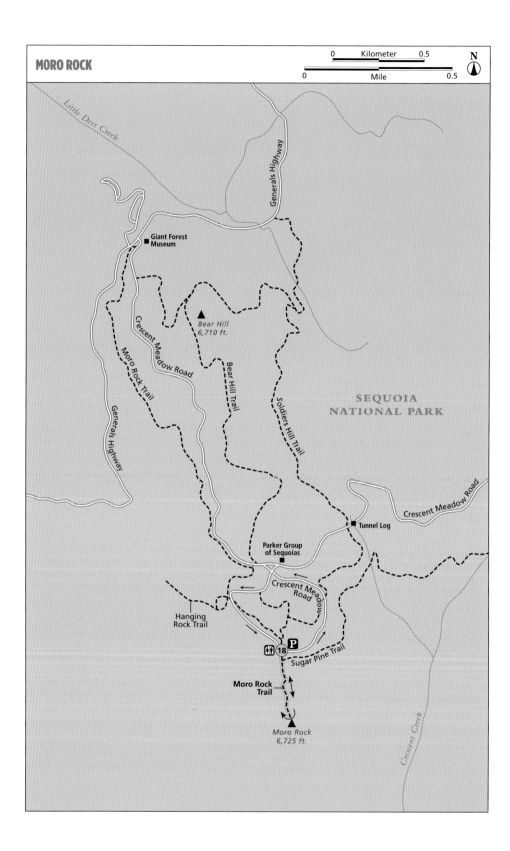

MORO ROCK

0   Kilometer   0.5
0   Mile   0.5

N

Little Deer Creek

Generals Highway

Giant Forest Museum

Crescent Meadow Road

Moro Rock Trail

Bear Hill Trail

▲ Bear Hill
6,710 ft.

Soldiers Hill Trail

SEQUOIA
NATIONAL PARK

Generals Highway

Crescent Meadow Road

■ Tunnel Log

Parker Group
of Sequoias ■

Crescent Meadow
Road

Hanging
Rock Trail

🚻 18 P

Sugar Pine Trail

Moro Rock
Trail

▲ Moro Rock
6,725 ft.

Crescent Creek

Left: Narrow passageways cut through the rock add excitement as the summit draws near.
Right: The dizzying view of the Moro Rock Trail as viewed from above.

If it's a busy day on the trail, you may need to wait your family's turn to walk out between the final guide rails here to the panoramic viewpoint. When you do, there will likely be many passers-by ready to take your family's photo with the view in exchange for your snapping theirs (so much better than trying to cram everyone in a selfie that won't show the view). Informational signs here help identify additional landmarks, including Sawtooth Peak, Castle Rocks, and Paradise Peak to the south.

While the return trip down along the same route will be far less challenging for the legs, remind kids to take their time and keep hold of the guardrails when using the stairs ('tis no place for a tumble), and go in front of them if possible to set the example. If you thought the views of the landscape were impressive on the way up, your views of the Moro Rock Trail far beneath you (known to inspire vertigo) will surely impress you on your way back down!

MILES AND DIRECTIONS

0.0   Start at the trailhead.

0.5   Arrive at the panoramic vista point. Double back when ready.

1.0   Return to the trailhead.

Late-day shade in Banshee Canyon,
Mojave National Preserve.

CALIFORNIA DESERTS

To those with little experience in them, any mention of "deserts" may paint the picture of vast, barren wastelands best experienced from the comfort of an air-conditioned car. Yet the deserts of California, when explored on foot, quickly prove to be anything but wastelands.

Even in the harsh conditions of Death Valley National Park, the hearty Salt Creek pupfish thrives in water several times saltier than the ocean. And in Anza-Borrego Desert State Park, not only do big-horn sheep roam the parched mountain slopes, but the spring wild-flowers put on such a widely anticipated show that they have their own hotline.

As you explore the 25 percent of California classified as desert, you'll discover distinctly different desert habitats, each with its own fascinating geology, flora, and fauna. In Joshua Tree National Park alone, you'll find two separate desert habitats. The western half is Mojave Desert habitat, where you'll hike among Joshua trees, prickly pear cacti, Mojave yucca, and pinyon pines. Yet the eastern half is actually Colorado Desert habitat (a part of the larger Sonoran Desert), with palo verde trees, spiky ocotillo, and enchanting teddy bear cholla.

These fourteen hikes, ranging from easy to strenuous, present prime examples of the wide-ranging desert landscapes and habitats to be found in California, including steep mountains, bizarre badlands, colorful canyons, palm-filled oases, dry falls, and even the miracle of a spring-fed desert waterfall.

Enjoy easy hiking with an iconic desert backdrop in this lesser-known California State Parks "Geological Gem."

Start: At the west edge of the parking area just off Abbott Drive
Elevation gain: 62 feet
Distance: 1.2-mile lollipop
Difficulty: Easy, with opportunities for scrambling and bouldering
Hiking time: About 45 minutes
Ages on foot: 3 years+
Seasons/schedule: Best in spring and fall; visitors center open limited days in summer and winter
Fees: Free to park at trailhead and hike, but visitors center (restrooms and water 3 minutes away) requires a day-use fee $$ or California Explorer Pass
Trail contact: California State Parks, Great Basin District, 15101 Lancaster Rd., Lancaster 93536, (661) 724-

1206, GreatBasin.District@parks.ca.gov
Trail surface: Dirt and sand
Land status: Natural preserve within a state park
Nearest town: Mojave
Dogs: Dogs not allowed on trails within Red Rock Canyon State Park
Maps: PDF map of Red Rock Canyon State Park and trails at www.parks.ca.gov/ and https://redrockrrcia.org/
Toilets: At the visitors center 0.9 mile north on Abbott Drive; day-use fee applies
Special considerations: Rattlesnakes, heat, and exposure. Wear excellent hats and sunglasses, and keep plenty of extra water in the car for refills when you're done.

FINDING THE TRAILHEAD

From the city of Mojave, drive 25 miles north on CA 14 and turn left onto Abbott Drive. The free, dirt parking area for Hagen Canyon will be immediately to your left (west). You'll find the signed trailhead at the west edge. **GPS:** N35 21.9' / W117 58.92'

THE HIKE

One of California's better-kept secrets, Red Rock Canyon State Park sits between the southernmost tip of the Sierra Nevada and the El Paso Range. Here you'll discover a vertical timeline dating back nearly 18 million years, shaped by tectonic thrusts, volcanic explosions, and a radically different climate that once brought an estimated 20 to 30 inches of rain to the region each year.

Starting west from the signed trailhead, follow the trail toward the rocky bluffs, imagining this area 10 million years ago when this was all beneath an ancient lake frequented by saber-toothed cats, three-toed horses, four-tusked elephants, and long-necked camels, whose rich deposits of fossils are found in the nearby Dove Springs Formation. You can see some at the visitors center.

Watch for the rocks lining both sides of the dirt path and small trail marker signs to help you stay on track, especially where you may cross or intercept a wash that also looks like a trail (and may have many shoe prints in it from those who have taken it instead).

At 0.1 mile stay to the right at the fork (southwest; you'll return on the other side of this loop), continuing on the side closer to the butte. As you proceed beneath the rocky butte, take in its vibrant layers and fantastical, rippling walls—sometimes called "curtains"—of sandstone.

Colorful Hagen Canyon captures the hiker's imagination.

Most of the deep red layers you'll see were once the bottoms of streams that flowed through here, with these sedimentary sand and rocky deposits containing higher levels of iron that now give the canyon its signature color. (During heavy winter rains, these red layers can appear to "bleed" down the canyon walls!)

At 0.3 mile look to your right (northwest) for Window Rock, which appears in an outcropping beneath the major butte. Here you can actually step inside a small room-like cave and enjoy the view from its "window." An unmarked trail cuts straight from your path up toward it and some marvelous bouldering for the more adventurous. When ready, return to the main path and continue southwest in your counterclockwise loop.

Be aware there are numerous offshoot trails through the brush from here, many following well-established washes for a while. If you decide to explore these, make sure your whole group is aware you're going off the main route, stays together, and knows to go slowly and be extra cautious about snakes. With younger children, it's recommended you

Top: The Rivoli kids looking out from Window Rock.
Bottom: Continue watching for the rock-lined designated trail and small markers throughout the preserve.

stick to the more wide-open, well-marked routes where it's easy to see what (and who) lies ahead on your path.

Between 0.6 and 0.7 mile you'll see trail markers pointing first straight, with a low outcropping to your left, then an arrow pointing left (south-southwest) where you'll suddenly see an opening between the rock formations. Pass through this gap and behold

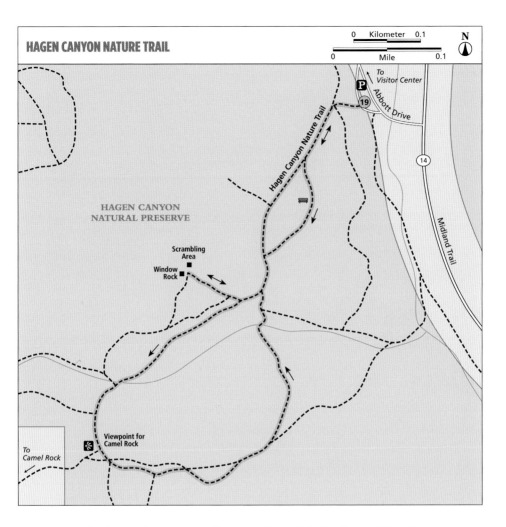

0   Kilometer   0.1

0   Mile   0.1

N

To
Visitor Center

P

19

Abbott Drive

14

Hagen Canyon Nature Trail

HAGEN CANYON
NATURAL PRESERVE

Midland Trail

Scrambling
Area

Window
Rock

Viewpoint for
Camel Rock

To
Camel Rock

spectacular desert views in every direction—it won't be hard to envision the many westerns and sci-fi films that borrowed these backdrops for their productions.

Stick with the rock-lined pathway, noting where it curves out to your right (west). Step into this unmarked "viewpoint," and look for the camel-colored Camel Rock rising in the distance with its funny face.

From here, you'll simply continue following the main route marked by its small rocks and occasional trail marker arrows, watching to your right (now south) for fantastical sand-castle–looking formations at 0.8 mile and mushroom-shaped structures at 0.9 mile. Just past these, take the left at the fork and look for the next trail marker that appears several steps up above your current path, inviting you to climb up a narrow, sandy path to the continuing trail.

This final stretch takes you through small Joshua trees with 360-degree views over the area you just hiked. Take a moment to rest on the bench here before finishing the gradually sloping walk back to the parking area and trailhead where you began.

Exploring the colorful and curious surfaces above Window Rock before returning to the main trail.

MILES AND DIRECTIONS

0.0   Starting at the trailhead, stay right at immediate fork (southwest).

0.3   Take right (northwest) side trail to Window Rock; return to main trail.

0.7   Follow trail marker to left (southwest).

0.9   Turn left at fork and continue up to the rise (northeast).

1.0   Take right fork (northeast) to follow eastern side of loop.

1.2   End back at trailhead.

(MOTION) PICTURE PERFECT

Since 1925, more than 150 movies and TV shows have been filmed in Red Rock Canyon State Park, including dozens of westerns, horror and sci-fi movies, and comedies. Some of the most famous movies filmed here include *The Mummy* (1933); *The Big Country* (1958); *The Long, Long Trailer* (1954); and *Jurassic Park* (1993). It's also been the backdrop for numerous popular TV shows, including *Battlestar Galactica*, *Bonanza*, *Lassie*, *Lost in Space*, and *Young Indiana Jones*.

20 DARWIN FALLS

This miracle-in-the-desert hike leads to one of the last things you might expect to find in Death Valley National Park: a year-round, spring-fed, 18-foot waterfall in an enchanting oasis frequented by dragonflies.

Start: At the signed trailhead (with map) at the south edge of the parking area

Elevation gain: 450 feet

Distance: 2-mile out-and-back

Difficulty: Easy to strenuous. Though it's usually labeled as an easy hike, that's true up until the first small waterfall. Between that and the main attraction it can get technical, including creek crossings, leaping from slippery rocks, and a steep rock face with a rope to help get up and down (details in hike description).

Hiking time: 1.5 to 2 hours

Ages on foot: 5 years+

Seasons/schedule: Oct through May

Fees: No fees required for this hike as it lies outside of the paid visiting boundary of Death Valley National Park

Trail contact: Death Valley National Park, PO Box 579, Death Valley 92328, (760) 786-3200

Trail surface: Dirt, rock, sand

Land status: National park

Nearest town: Panamint Springs

Dogs: No dogs

Toilets: None; nearest restrooms in private businesses in nearby Panamint Springs

Maps: In the Death Valley hiking section of the NPS app and at www.nps.gov/deva/

Special considerations: Slippery rocks at stream crossings and around the waterfall lead to many a wet shoe; those with knee issues will need to be extra cautious in the final approach to the falls.

FINDING THE TRAILHEAD

From the Olancha junction on US 395, take CA 190 East for 44 miles—watch your odometer. You will turn right (south) onto an unmarked dirt road 0.75 mile *before* Panamint Springs (look for the skinny water pipe to the left side as you start down this road shown on maps as "Old Toll Road"). A short way in, you will *then* see a faded brown sign for "Darwin Falls Road and Day Use Area." Continue 2.5 miles down this rugged dirt, gravel, and rocky road, which is generally passable in a non-four-wheel-drive as long as you are mindful of any outlier rocks. If coming from the park's east side on CA 190, just watch for the Panamint Spring Resort and gas station on your left (south), then continue 0.75 mile to the dirt road turn-off as described above. **GPS:** N36 19.66' / W117 30.88'

THE HIKE

The hike starts in lower Darwin Wash, most likely without a trace of water (which fluctuates here by the season), though you may already see hints of wildflowers scattered at the edges. Named for the 1850s prospector Dr. E. Darwin French (rather than Charles), it's easy to see why he chose this sheltered corridor for his base camp as you travel farther up canyon and the first puffs of desert willow appear along your route.

Here you'll likely begin to hear the first significant trickles of water on this hike. If you step closer to the water-loving willows and brush that line the creek, you may be able to enjoy some shade from overhanging trees as you pause for a water break. If your family

The hidden grotto of Darwin Falls
in Death Valley National Park.

Top: The brush and wildflowers thicken as you stumble onto the first water in Darwin Wash.
Bottom: The Rivoli kids help each other in scaling the large boulder with a rope.

hasn't already started watching for lizards, now is the time. You may easily spot four or more varieties between here and the final waterfall!

Between 0.7 and 0.8 mile, the canyon begins narrowing as the fine-leafed trees hang farther overhead, creating a completely different atmosphere from where your adventure began. Note how the air feels different and the foliage thickens, creating a verdant riparian retreat with a cattail-lined creek beside you and a small waterfall splashing from behind it.

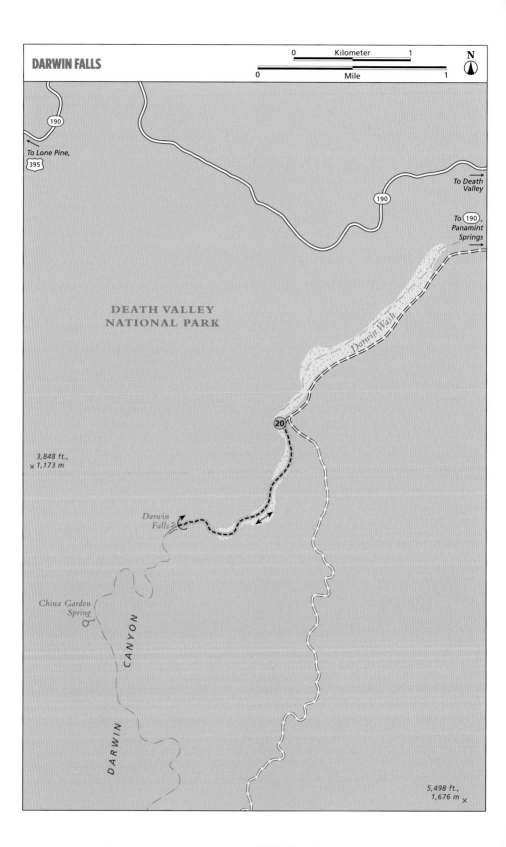

DARWIN FALLS

0   Kilometer   1
0   Mile   1

N

190

To Lone Pine,
395

190

To Death
Valley

To 190,
Panamint
Springs

DEATH VALLEY
NATIONAL PARK

Darwin Wash

20

3,848 ft.,
× 1,173 m

Darwin
Falls

China Garden
Spring

CANYON

DARWIN

5,498 ft.,
1,676 m ×

Scarlet red dragonflies and bright blue damselflies collect in the cool shade at Darwin Falls.

Soon the creek-crossings begin, where you may find any manner of rocks or cut branches lain across the water to assist you—but don't count on them not to move beneath your feet! (At least one pair of wet shoes is to be expected by the end of this family hike.) Just remember any rocks you leap to with wet shoes will be extra slippery upon landing. At 0.9 mile you'll cross a short, narrow footbridge (as wide as a shoe) just before arriving at the first and smaller waterfall. Pass along to the right side of it, and get ready for more rigorous climbing.

Depending on the timing of your visit, it may be easiest to go up and over the rather steep rocky section of trail to your right (north) or to clamber up the large rocky slope where you may see fellow hikers using a rope to assist. If the water is very low, you may have additional options depending on your creativity and willingness to get your shoes wet.

But the reward just ahead will be clear once the Eiffel Tower–shaped waterfall comes into view and you step into the grotto of Darwin Falls. Take some time to soak up the scenery and sounds—it's a place unlike any other you'll experience in Death Valley National Park.

When ready, reverse course and return to the trailhead.

MILES AND DIRECTIONS

0.0   Start at the Darwin Falls trailhead.

1.0   Reach Darwin Falls.

2.0   Arrive back at the trailhead.

21 SALT CREEK

If you visit in winter through spring, this easy boardwalk trail takes you through a most unusual sight to behold in Death Valley—flowing water filled with fish!

Start: Signed trailhead where wooden boardwalk begins at west end of parking area
Elevation gain: 26 feet
Distance: 0.8-mile lollipop (or more if you take spur trail)
Difficulty: Easy
Hiking time: 25 minutes+ (depends on how long you spend at interpretive signs)
Ages on foot: 2 years+
Seasons/schedule: Nov through May when water still flows to this area; best Feb through Apr when pupfish are spawning
Fees: Weekly vehicle pass $$$$, annual national parks pass, or Every Kid Outdoors Pass (*free* for fourth graders)

Trail contact: Death Valley National Park, PO Box 579, Death Valley 92328, (760) 786-3200
Trail surface: Mostly wooden boardwalk and an optional sand/dirt spur trail
Land status: National park
Nearest town: Stovepipe Wells
Dogs: No dogs
Toilets: At parking area
Maps: Map at trailhead kiosk (though not needed if you just stay on boardwalk trail)
Special considerations: Heat and exposure, otherwise minimal if you stay on boardwalk trail, which is stroller- and wheelchair-friendly
Gear suggestions: Umbrella for shade (easy to carry along this easy but exposed trail)

FINDING THE TRAILHEAD

From Stovepipe Wells take CA 190 east for 11 miles; or from Furnace Creek, drive west for 13 miles. Turn west (then continue southwest) at the sign for Salt Creek, and follow the dirt and semi-washboard gravel road approximately 1 mile to the parking area. The wooden boardwalk begins at the first informational sign you'll see at the west end of the parking area. **GPS:** N36 35.4' / W116 59.4'

THE HIKE

The hearty pupfish of Salt Creek have a history dating back more than 10,000 years, to a time when a great freshwater lake filled today's Death Valley Basin. As many rivers of the Ice Age diminished throughout this region, so too did the 620-acre Lake Manly. The pupfish population was left scattered between different, disconnected bodies of water, from Mono Lake in the north to the ancient Mojave Lake in today's San Bernardino County.

As time passed, ten different species of pupfish evolved in their different locations, with two now extinct. The Salt Creek pupfish is perhaps the most unlikely survivor of all of these—having adapted to living in water several times as salty as seawater, and with many of them making *only* the one-way, 1-mile journey from the creek's brackish springwater source to this protected area flowing beside (and through) the boardwalk.

The flow of water gradually decreases from winter to spring, leaving extremely shallow and even disconnected stretches of Salt Creek where the pupfish can become easy targets for wildlife. By late summer, most of this lower portion of the creek dries completely

Visit Death Valley's rare residents thriving in water several times saltier than the ocean.

Top: Informational signs are found throughout the educational boardwalk loop.
Bottom: As you cross the bridge look to the nearby hills for traces of fossilized animal tracks.

from the harsh summer heat. The sole survivors from this section will be the pupfish who bury themselves in the mud of the deepest lingering pools where they'll hibernate until summer is past.

As you follow the trail in its counterclockwise loop, enjoy the informational displays illustrating the plight of the pupfish, the intriguing adaptations of the plants surviving in the salty soil and heat here, and the prehistoric residents whose fossils are found in hills surrounding the creek.

SALT CREEK

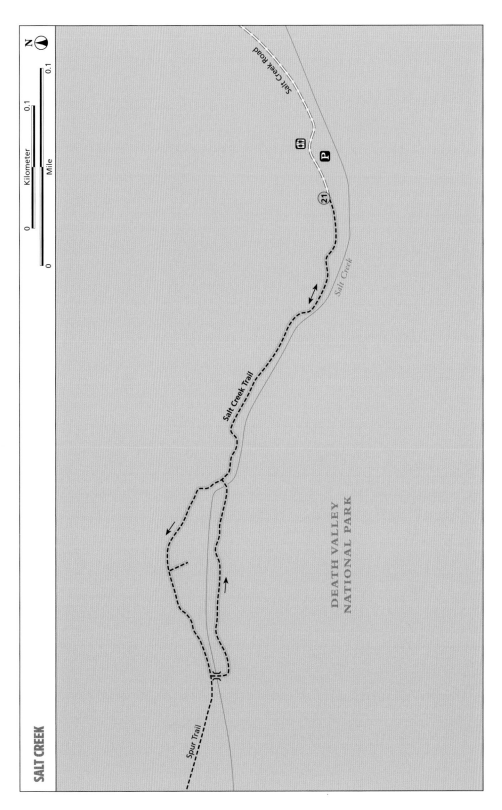

Salt Creek Road

21

P

Salt Creek Trail

Salt Creek

DEATH VALLEY
NATIONAL PARK

Spur Trail

N

Kilometer
0   0.1   0.1

Mile
0   0.1

Tiny but mighty, the salt creek pupfish has adapted and outlasted mastodons.

MILES AND DIRECTIONS

0.0   Start at the trailhead at the beginning of the boardwalk.

0.2   Turn right at the fork.

0.4   Cross a wooden bridge and continue left on the main boardwalk (south, then west), or explore the sandy spur trail to the right (west) first, adding about 0.2 mile out and back.

0.8   Arrive back at the trailhead.

22 GOLDEN CANYON TO RED CATHEDRAL

Feast your eyes on the best of Death Valley's badlands from the glowing depths of Golden Canyon to the unforgettable views from trail's end at Red Cathedral.

Start: Signed trailhead for Golden Canyon
Elevation gain: 577 feet
Distance: 3-mile out-and-back
Difficulty: Moderate to strenuous, with some minor rock scrambling, ducking under low overhangs, and steep incline with slippery soil to complete full hike
Hiking time: 1.5 to 2 hours
Ages on foot: 5 years for Golden Canyon, 7+ for Red Cathedral portion
Seasons/schedule: Nov through Apr, hike early to avoid full-sun exposure near midday and extra high temperatures in the radiant canyon in the afternoon
Fees: Weekly vehicle pass $$$$, annual national parks pass, or Every Kid Outdoors Pass (*free* for fourth graders)
Trail contact: Death Valley National Park, PO Box 579, Death Valley 92328, (760) 786-3200

Trail surface: Dirt, rock, sand, and gravel
Land status: National park
Nearest town: Furnace Creek
Dogs: No dogs
Toilets: At trailhead
Maps: See printable map for "Golden Canyon, Gower Gulch, and Badlands" at www.nps.gov/deva/ and overview map at trailhead
Special considerations: The final Red Cathedral portion gets very steep (can cause vertigo for some) and has no railings; the surfaces can be slippery when dry. It's recommended only for children who will exercise caution. Precipitation here is a risk to anyone, so the canyon should never be entered during the rare chance of a rain event.
Gear suggestions: Hiking shoes with good traction for the technical portions and excellent sun hat and/or travel umbrella to make your own shade in the exposed canyon.

FINDING THE TRAILHEAD

From Furnace Creek drive 1 mile east on CA 190; or from Death Valley Junction, drive 29 miles west on CA 190. Turn south at the junction with Badwater Road and drive another 2 miles. Turn left (east) into the signed Golden Cathedral trailhead parking area immediately off Badwater Road. **GPS:** N36 25.08' / W118 50.82'

THE HIKE

To get maximum enjoyment from this hike (richest colors, contrasting textures, and manageable temperatures), start in early morning at the Golden Canyon trailhead just off Badwater Road. Shortly after entering Golden Canyon, morning sidelight sets the surrounding tawny siltstones and mudstones aglow.

As you venture into the gently inclining wash of Golden Canyon, look for remnants of the old road on which motorists traveled into this canyon until February of 1976, when a four-day rainstorm culminated in a flash flooding event that washed most of it away. It's a powerful example of what only 2.3 inches of rain can do in a desert canyon—especially in a location accustomed to an average of only 1.65 inches per year.

Morning hikers enter Golden Canyon as it's set aglow by the rising sun.

Next, look around for hints of an ancient desert lakebed, with its diagonal stripes of sedimentary layers thrust up at odd angles over time. As you follow the twists and turns of the main canyon, you'll pass a number of unmarked (and unmapped) narrow canyons leading off to each side. While these can be enticing to curious kids and adults alike, be sure everyone in your group knows not to venture into these unless it's all together going in—and coming back out.

Between the jagged cliffs flow the softer badlands slopes of mudstones and silt, which contain evaporites like the borax once hauled by the legendary twenty-mule teams of Death Valley. In good lighting you'll see a variety of colors among these, from buff to mustard and even some shades of green.

A steep climb with a little scrambling leads you up the final stretch of Red Cathedral to a spectacular view awaiting above.

At 1 mile you'll arrive at Red Cathedral Junction, noted by a sign at the right (east) edge of the wide wash, where an opening in the canyon wall gives way to the trails to Zabriskie Point and Gower Gulch. Continue straight (northeast) on the wide, main wash as your own path narrows and the spectacle of Red Cathedral and its rippling russet wall begins rising dramatically above.

Begin your gradual climb up some large rocks, with a shimmy and squeeze up through a narrow rock opening as well. Suddenly you'll find yourselves standing beneath the

GOLDEN CANYON TO RED CATHEDRAL

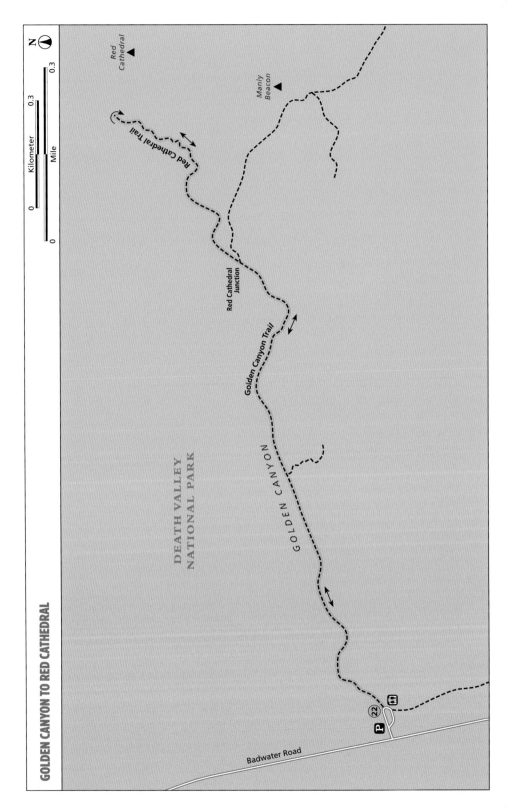

N

Kilometer
0   0.3

Mile
0   0.3

Red Cathedral

Manly Beacon

Red Cathedral Trail

Red Cathedral Junction

Golden Canyon Trail

DEATH VALLEY NATIONAL PARK

GOLDEN CANYON

Badwater Road

P 22

The hike's grand finale in early morning light reveals the striking colors and textures seen from Red Cathedral, with a view across Death Valley all the way to the Panamint Mountains.

600-foot face of Red Cathedral. Follow the worn trail as it steepens, taking care with the loose, sandy surface as you finally arrive at an exposed overlook (no railings and the same slippery trail surface) and the final 10 feet of this trail. (Those with a fear of heights or vertigo should wait below.)

Have a seat and enjoy this spectacular view over Golden Canyon, out over Death Valley itself, with the Panamint Mountains in the distance (if you started early enough, you'll also enjoy shade here while you rest). When ready, make your extremely cautious exit back down from this vantage point—scooting on your backside if needed. Then follow your tracks back to the trailhead where you began, enjoying the benefit of the gradual decline on your return.

MILES AND DIRECTIONS

0.0 Start at the Golden Canyon Trailhead.

1.0 At Red Cathedral Junction, continue straight (northeast).

1.5 Arrive at the end point and savor the view from Red Cathedral. Retrace your steps.

3.0 Arrive back at the trailhead.

Hikers pass through layers of an ancient lakebed thrust up at angles over time.

23 NATURAL BRIDGE CANYON

Enjoy a short hike to one of the most photographed landmarks in Death Valley, the 35-foot-high and equally deep Natural Bridge. Then continue upcanyon to a scramble-worthy dry fall at trail's end.

Start: Signed trailhead at east end of parking area
Elevation gain: 450 feet
Distance: 1.4-mile out-and-back
Difficulty: Moderate because of continuous elevation gain on the outbound leg, with radiant canyon heat most days from mid-morning on
Hiking time: 45 minutes to 1 hour (possibly longer with scrambling enthusiasts and lizard hunters)
Ages on foot: 4 years+
Seasons/schedule: Nov through Apr, hike early to avoid full-sun exposure near midday and extra high temperatures in the radiant canyon in the afternoon
Fees and permits: Weekly vehicle pass $$$$, annual national parks pass, or Every Kid Outdoors Pass (*free* for fourth graders)

Trail contact: Death Valley National Park, PO Box 579, Death Valley 92328, (760) 786-3200
Trail surface: Dirt, rock, and gravel
Land status: National park
Nearest town: Furnace Creek
Dogs: No dogs
Toilets: At trailhead
Maps: No official trail as you simply follow the canyon wash, though there is an overview map at the trailhead.
Special considerations: Heat, exposure, and slipping/falling if climbing the dry fall at the end of the trail (polished/worn rock coated in slippery dust requires careful attention)
Gear suggestions: Umbrella for shade if needed and grippy-soled hiking shoes to scramble around the dry fall.

FINDING THE TRAILHEAD

From Furnace Creek drive 1 mile east on CA 190; or from Death Valley Junction, drive 29 miles west on CA 190. Turn south at the junction for Badwater Road and drive 13.5 miles to the left (east) at the sign for "Natural Bridge." Follow this exciting, graded dirt road (usually passable by sedans—keep moving!) for about 1 mile, quickly gaining elevation up the side of an alluvial fan to the designated parking area. The trailhead awaits at the east end of the parking area, marked by an informational kiosk with map. **GPS:** N36 16.8' / W116 46.14'

THE HIKE

Before setting out up the trail, take a moment to look at the multisided information kiosk at the trailhead, which provides a good overview of how the canyon and its namesake arch likely formed.

The first stretch of the hike is, admittedly, lackluster with plentiful elevation gain and the best view—for the time being—behind you. But once you reach the mouth of the canyon, things get interesting. Look up for signs of small, natural gutters notched by rain along the top of the canyon wall, where early morning hikers may even see condensation collected from the cool night's air. And take a close look at the jagged canyon walls, made from a combination of rock, gravel, and sediment that was washed to the base of an ancient mountain 3 to 5 million years ago.

Four Rivoli family hikers pass beneath the iconic arch of Death Valley.

Don't miss the petite "Cathedral of the Dry Chute" just beyond the main attraction.

Over the thousands of years that followed, infrequent but powerful flash-flooding events carved this canyon and several others like it here in the western side of Death Valley's Black Mountains. You can see evidence of their courses changing over time as you travel up the canyon wash. During one of these historic course changes, the turbulent waters began wearing a hole through the lower rock to form the unmistakable Natural Bridge you'll pass beneath at 0.4 mile.

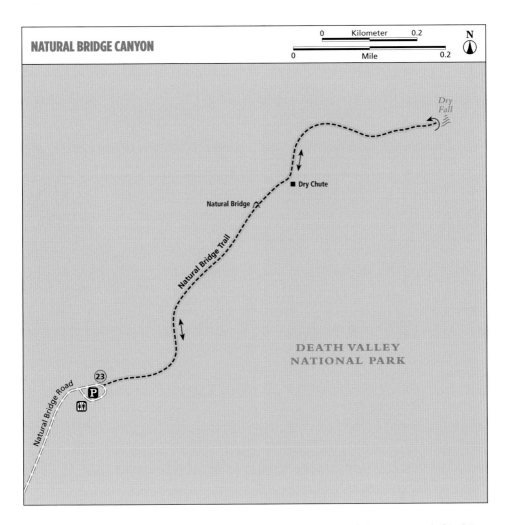

From here, you'll begin leaving the majority of visitors and their cameras behind. Just 0.1 mile farther up the trail, look to your right (southeast) for a dry waterfall. This marvelous, vertical chute is set back from the trail in what feels to some like a petite stone cathedral (go ahead and check the acoustics if you're feeling bold).

As you continue upcanyon, the gravelly wash bends left (northwest) and this is the time to look in the same direction for a spooky-looking cave set high in the canyon wall. In this quieter portion of the canyon, you may begin to see more signs of desert life, including minor vegetation and lizards sunning (or shading) themselves along the larger rocks.

At 0.7 mile the otherwise colorful canyon appears to dead-end in a 15-foot dry fall of weather-polished gray bedrock. If your family wants to explore these, scramble with care as the natural steps can be quite slippery (grippy-soled hiking shoes recommended).

When ready, reverse course back to the trailhead, enjoying views of the Death Valley Basin stretching all the way to the Panamint Mountains on your return.

Left: Slippery when dry: The 15-foot dry fall at the end is best explored with caution—and grippy-soled shoes.
Right: Enjoy canyon-framed views across Death Valley as you return to the trailhead.

MILES AND DIRECTIONS

- **0.0**   Start at the trailhead.
- **0.4**   Go under the Natural Bridge.
- **0.5**   Reach the dry chute.
- **0.7**   Arrive at the dry waterfall (end point).
- **1.4**   Return to the trailhead.

24 BADWATER SALT FLAT

This salt-flat stroll over the lowest of the lowlands on the North American continent gives you a memorable perspective of Death Valley and some fun photo ops.

Start: Information signs at viewing platform at west edge of parking area
Elevation gain: 6 feet (mostly the steps or ramp down)
Distance: 1.5-mile+ (as desired and depending on the heat) out-and-back
Difficulty: Easy, except for the likely heat and exposure
Hiking time: 45 minutes to 1 hour
Ages on foot: 2 years+
Seasons/schedule: Nov through Apr
Fees: Weekly vehicle pass $$$$, annual national parks pass, or Every Kid Outdoors Pass (*free* for fourth graders and their families)
Trail contact: Death Valley National Park, PO Box 579, Death Valley 92328, (760) 786-3200

Trail surface: Dirt, rock, and gravel
Land status: National park
Nearest town: Furnace Creek
Dogs: No dogs
Toilets: At parking area
Maps: No official trail as you simply follow the canyon wash, though there is an overview map at the trailhead.
Special considerations: Sun exposure and heat. Ramps and boardwalk area are stroller- and wheelchair-friendly.
Gear suggestions: Excellent sunglasses and sunblock as the light reflecting off the white salt can be extremely bright (and reflects UV up under sun hats)

FINDING THE TRAILHEAD

From Furnace Creek drive 1 mile east on CA 190; or from Death Valley Junction, drive 29 miles west on CA 190. Turn south at the junction with Badwater Road and drive 17 miles to the highly visible parking area on the right (west) side of the road. Start at the viewing platform and follow either the steps or accessible ramp down to the boardwalk to start your adventure. **GPS:** N36 15' / W'116 49.2'

THE HIKE

Start at the viewing platform above the salt flat to help orient yourselves and get an overview of the vast salt flats—nearly 200 square miles—that were once the bottom of ancient Lake Manly. With no outlet for the lake's water, high concentrations of sediment including salt and borax built up over time and remained when the waters dried up.

Once you arrive at the boardwalk area, be sure to stroll over to the spring-fed pool just to the north of it. Here you'll see fascinating proof that even in this harsh, hot, and saline environment, life can adapt—and even thrive. Cases in point: The flourishes of pickleweed found around this pool and its resident Badwater snail (*Angustassiminea infima*), a salt marsh snail existing only in this strange location. (Be sure your family sticks to the boardwalk and stays out of their habitat here.)

As you make your way beyond the boardwalk onto the dazzling, snow-white surface of the salt flat itself, be sure to stay on the well-worn pathway (aka already crushed) route to avoid unnecessary damage to the surrounding area. Now, take a moment to turn back toward the parking area and Black Mountains behind it, and look for the sign on a cliff

Walking west toward the Panamint Mountains on Badwater Basin salt flat.

above indicating "Sea Level." Your family is now standing 282 feet below the ocean's surface, on the lowest point in the North American continent. And if that's not reason enough to snap a commemorative photo, the surface you're standing on looks like snow!

While you can backtrack to the trailhead at any time (and certainly do so if the heat is feeling intense at this point), it's a joy to leave the busiest area behind and venture a little farther into this vast, surreal expanse. The farther you go, the more likely you will get a good view of the naturally occurring salt polygons that form here as groundwater seeps up through the saline soil in undisturbed areas off the trail. Squint your eyes slightly to help reveal the linoleum-like repeating pattern of raised salt-encrusted edges.

The spring-fed pool with reflections of the Black Mountains, as first seen from the parking overlook.

Kindly stay on the established route! The geometric salt polygon designs get trampled with every visitor stepping a little farther off the worn trail to get the best detail photo.

However far you comfortably trek out onto Badwater Basin, take a moment to size up the mountains before you—and behind you, too—before your return. At the west edge of this basin, the Panamint Mountains rise rapidly, with their highest point of Telescope Peak (11,049 feet) towering more than 2 miles above you—one of the greatest, visible vertical reliefs one can see at such close range in North America.

As you head back to the trailhead, survey the Black Mountains rising behind the parking area. The nearest, highest point is Dante's Peak—where you may find yourselves hiking soon and watching tiny little ant-like hikers, such as yourselves, moving over the white salt flat.

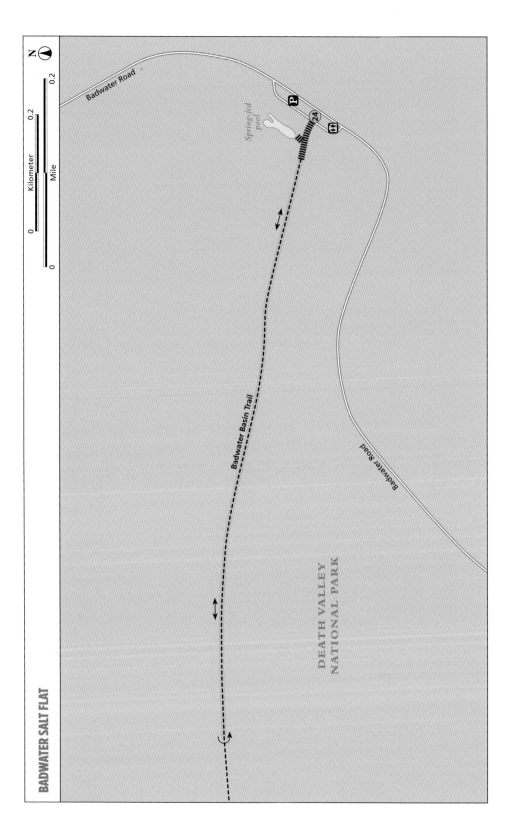

BADWATER SALT FLAT

Badwater Road

Spring-fed pool

Badwater Basin Trail

Badwater Road

DEATH VALLEY
NATIONAL PARK

N

Kilometer
0   0.2

Mile
0   0.2

That's not snow on the ground—but there is still late spring snow seen on Telescope Peak, towering 2 miles above the basin.

The journey starts at the bustling boardwalk section and improves with distance.

MILES AND DIRECTIONS

0.0	Start at the trailhead.
0.1	Leave the boardwalk to continue on the informal trail.
0.7 to 1.0	Turn back when ready.
1.5+	Return to trailhead.

25 DANTE'S PEAK

This short, sweet hike takes you to an unforgettable vantage point over Death Valley with panoramic views over the park including its lowest point beneath you and highest point straight across the valley itself.

Start: From the dirt trail leading from the north end of the viewing area
Elevation gain: 249 feet
Distance: 1-mile out-and-back, with scenic spurs
Difficulty: Moderate (starting at high elevation for most, with rugged tripping rocks and sand and climbing over some tricky spots and up to views)
Hiking time: About 45 minutes
Ages on foot: 5 years+
Seasons/schedule: Oct through May, come in early morning for the best lighting over the dramatic landscape
Fees: Weekly vehicle pass $$$$, annual national parks pass, or Every Kid Outdoors Pass (*free* for fourth graders)
Trail contact: Death Valley National Park, PO Box 579, Death Valley 92328, (760) 786-3200
Trail surface: Gravel, dirt, rocks
Land status: National park

Nearest town: Furnace Creek
Dogs: No dogs on any trails in Death Valley National Park
Toilets: At turnout 0.5 mile before reaching this parking area
Maps: NPS App map for Death Valley, park visitors map, and online at www.nps.gov/deva/
Special considerations: Rugged rocks to step over, uneven and slippery loose dirt sections, potential tripping hazards, and steep drop-offs with no safety rails. There is also the possibility of rattlesnakes (just ask my kids), so pay attention to rocks and brush near the trail as well as the amazing views.
Gear suggestions: Jackets or windbreakers, and hats with lanyards or sweatshirts with hoods. At its higher elevation, Dante's View is generally much cooler than other popular stops in the park and can be quite breezy.

FINDING THE TRAILHEAD

From Furnace Creek drive east on CA 190 for 12 miles; or from Death Valley Junction, drive west on CA 190 for 18 miles. Turn south onto the signed Dante's View Road for a memorable 13.3-mile drive up the steep, winding road to Dante's View parking area. If needed, be sure to stop at the restrooms about 0.5 mile before the parking area as there are no restrooms at the top. **GPS:** N36 13.24' / W116 43.6'

THE HIKE

Before your hike, take a look at the interpretive displays in the official viewing area to help get oriented with where you are in the park geographically and also where you are located within the western United States.

Most visitors who make it to this point are satisfied with this lofty overlook, while others venture out to the lower, shorter lookout trail southwest of this area. Your adventurous family, however, will proceed to the north end of the viewing area and continue on the unmarked, but well-established, dirt trail that quickly leads up toward the higher ground of Dante's Peak.

Follow the trail as it curves to the left (west) side of the mountain, giving you even better views over Death Valley, and keep younger children especially close as you proceed along this next section where they may need help navigating over or around some large, jagged rocks (and there is no guardrail or safety fence at any point on this trail).

At 0.2 mile you'll see a spur trail heading over to a "natural balcony" from which those without a fear of heights may enjoy a truly unique view of Badwater Salt Flat, a small white stripe visible far below with tiny moving spots of—yes, those are people walking on the Salt Flat.

Soon, you'll encounter the first of several short, informal connector trails leading up to the summit ridge and truly panoramic views. (Go up or down with your kids only if and where you feel comfortable as these are optional.) Continue north until you arrive at the wide-open space of the 5,704-foot peak itself, and see if your kids can find the USGS marker to prove it.

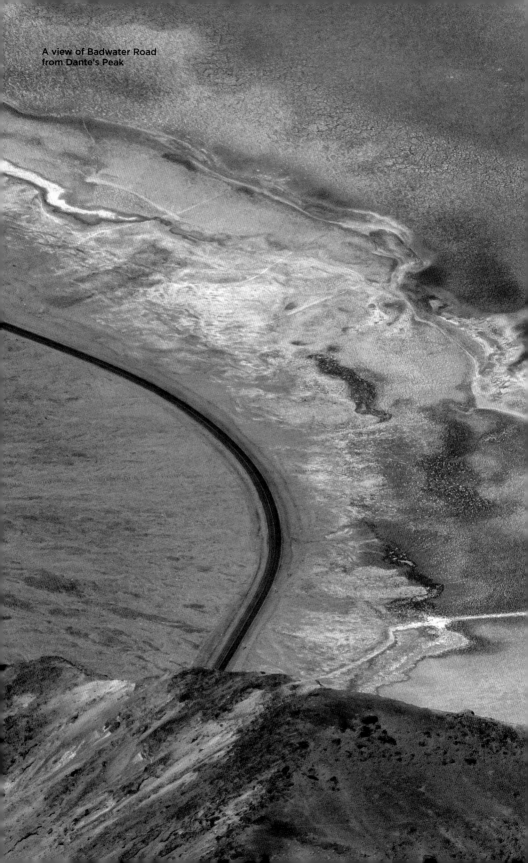

A view of Badwater Road
from Dante's Peak

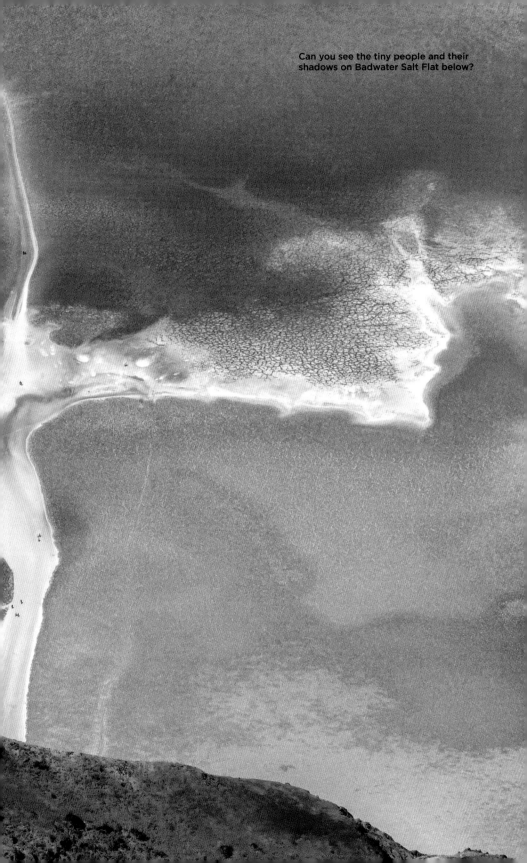

Can you see the tiny people and their shadows on Badwater Salt Flat below?

Top: A view over Death Valley Basin with a lightly snow-topped Telescope Peak in the distance. Bottom: Return view of the trail (left) with bonus trail leading southwest from the viewing area to the right.

To the west, across the otherworldly expanse of the Death Valley Basin, you'll see the Panamint Range rising dramatically with Telescope Peak, the highest point in the park (at 11,049 feet), directly across from you and only 12 miles away.

On the clearest days, it's possible to see both the lowest point in North America and the highest point in the contiguous United States from this vantage point. In addition to Badwater Basin below, Mount Whitney may also be visible to the northwest of Telescope Peak, where it rises to 14,505 feet in the Sierra Nevada.

Enjoy the views and, when ready, reverse course and return to the trailhead.

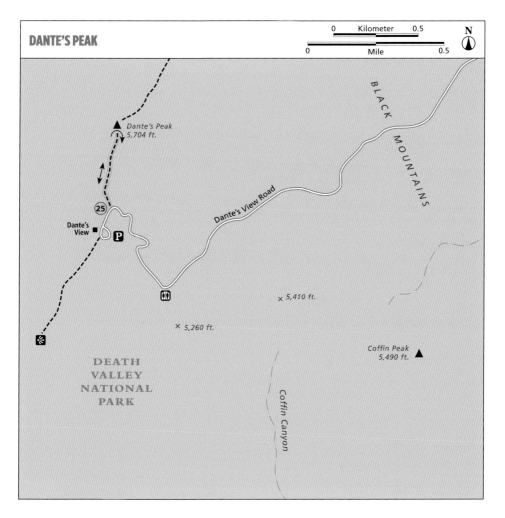

DANTE'S PEAK

0 Kilometer 0.5
0 Mile 0.5
N

Dante's Peak
5,704 ft.

25

Dante's View

P

Dante's View Road

BLACK MOUNTAINS

× 5,410 ft.

× 5,260 ft.

Coffin Peak
5,490 ft.

DEATH
VALLEY
NATIONAL
PARK

Coffin Canyon

MILES AND DIRECTIONS

- **0.0**   Start at the trailhead.
- **0.2**   Take the left (west) spur trail to an overlook; return to main trail.
- **0.3**   **Optional:** Take connector trail to right (east) to reach parallel ridge trail above
- **0.5**   Arrive at Dante's Peak.
- **1.0**   Return to the trailhead.

IN A GALAXY FAR, FAR AWAY . . .

The scenic overlook at Dante's View was used as a filming location in the 1977 movie *Star Wars*. It was from this vantage point that the characters looked out over the spaceport of Mos Eisley—painted "into" this scene by talented matte artists.

26 RINGS LOOP

In a mere 1.5 miles, you'll encounter classic Mojave Desert scenery, prehistoric petroglyphs, a cathedral-like canyon, and the thrill of a narrow slot-canyon exit up a series of rock-mounted climbing rings.

Start: At the signed trailhead at the south end of the parking area—opposite the Hole-in-the-Wall Visitors Center (see note in hike description)
Elevation gain: 144 feet
Distance: 1.5-mile loop
Difficulty: Easy for the first mile, then moderate/strenuous with scrambling up boulders and climbing up the rings to exit Banshee Canyon
Hiking time: 1 hour
Ages on foot: 5 years+ (for climbing rings with some assistance)
Seasons/schedule: Best Mar through May and Oct through Nov
Fees: Free
Trail contact: Mojave National Preserve, 2701 Barstow Rd., Barstow 92311, (760) 252-6100
Trail surface: Dirt and rock
Land status: National preserve

Nearest town: Essex
Dogs: Pets on leash are allowed on all trails in Mojave National Preserve; however, even the most agile of the species may not be able to climb the rings loop portion of this hike, so you would need to double back from there.
Toilets: At trailhead
Maps: On display at trailhead
Special considerations: Rattlesnakes, so urge caution for young hikers (no running) and stay together on the main trail where visibility is best. Be ready for sun exposure and heat; bring more water than you expect to need on the trail and have extra waiting in the car. There are no concessions in Mojave National Preserve, so bring everything you'll want to eat and drink with you.

FINDING THE TRAILHEAD

If traveling from the north (e.g., Baker), your navigation system may try to route you through the preserve, rather than routing you around to this entrance from the south and I-40. Unless you have a rugged vehicle, full-size spare, and an appetite for 16 miles of driving over rugged/washboard gravel and dirt roads without cell reception or signs of human life for the most part, you'll want to enter Mojave National Preserve from the south. Also, there is no gas within Mojave National Preserve, so be sure to top off your tank before entering.

From Barstow, drive 100 miles east on I-40 / Needles Freeway, or from Needles drive 41 miles west. Take exit 100 for Essex Road, and proceed 20 miles north to Black Canyon Road. Make a slight right onto Black Canyon Road and continue 10 miles, following signs to the Hole-in-the-Wall Visitors Center, where you'll park and start at the signed trailhead at the south end of the parking area, not beside the visitor center (where you will end). **GPS:** N35 2.52' / W115 24'

THE HIKE

From the signed trailhead at the south end of the visitor center parking area, head south on the dirt path with the rocky butte to your right (it remains to your right during most of this clockwise loop). For this first section, families may want to walk in the wider wash running parallel to the trail, where visibility is best. **Caution:** Keep an eye out for rattlesnakes.

An easy hike turns challenging when you arrive at two sets of climbing rings leading you up dry waterfalls and out of Banshee Canyon.

At 0.1 mile proceed through the first of two narrow, barbed-wire fence pass-throughs, and continue on, following the dirt trail around the base of the rocky butte. Enjoy the expansive view of Wildhorse Canyon as it opens up to the west with desert hills and Wildhorse Mesa in the distance.

Watch for the informational sign at 0.4 mile, where you'll have the chance to step off the main trail and get up close to large boulders featuring ancient petroglyphs. Who will

A close-up view of prehistoric petroglyphs on the Rings Loop Trail.

be the first to spot a bighorn sheep?! Make sure to approach the boulders with caution and care so you don't startle any resting desert wildlife.

While little is known about the makers of the prehistoric rock art, the style has been dubbed "Great Basin Curvilinear Abstract," and this site is one of the precious few in the area that has not suffered vandalism. This artwork, created by chipping away at the darker "desert varnish" layer of the rocks, is believed to date back thousands of years before the two earliest culture groups known to inhabit the area: the Mojave and the Chemehuevi.

Continuing on the main trail, rounding the butte, your view reveals more desert hills and a small mesa in the distance. Watch for the unique outcropping high on the rocks to your right (north) with natural caves that give the appearance of prehistoric cliffside dwellings (not known to have been so for humans, but surely many other desert-dwelling creatures over time).

At 0.8 mile you'll pass through the second barbed-wire fence openings and continue rounding beneath the butte as a tall mesa appears straight ahead of you. As you get closer, keep an eye out for the first *holes in the wall*, both in the stony surfaces ahead of you and to your right.

Rather than a solitary "hole in the wall," you'll see a Swiss-cheese network of circular pocks evidencing the violent volcanic past of this area some 16–18 million years ago. The signature formations at Hole in the Rock are ancient gas bubbles (or "vesicles") that formed as the magma cooled more quickly than they could escape and that have been revealed by weather and time.

At 1 mile the trail leads you over and through large rocks and boulders to a narrow opening between the towering, 200-foot walls into Banshee Canyon. If you follow along the steep wall directly ahead of you toward your right, you'll find a dry waterfall tucked

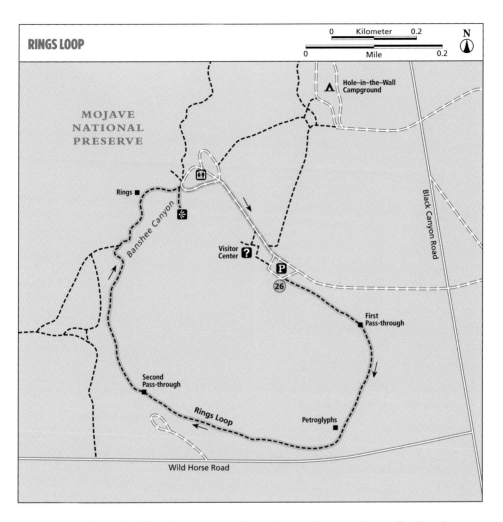

0   Kilometer   0.2

0   Mile   0.2

N

MOJAVE
NATIONAL
PRESERVE

Hole–in–the–Wall
Campground

Rings ■

Banshee Canyon

Black Canyon Road

Visitor
Center ?

P

26

First
Pass-through ■

Second
Pass-through ■

Rings Loop

Petroglyphs ■

Wild Horse Road

into a niche, which is an interesting sight on its own, but it is also outfitted with a rope for the daring to practice climbing against the fall. **Caution:** Do so at your own risk.

At the left end of this wall, the trail appears to end in a pile of boulders (which may or may not have a weathered arrow sign above them during your visit indicating the way out). Scramble up the boulders until a narrow slot canyon appears to your right and, with it, the first set of climbing rings.

For most it will work best to use the rings as handholds and the rings' mounting stems as footrests as you climb (rather than putting your feet in the rings). Once you've cleared the first and longest set of rings, you'll climb up the second and narrowest set (cinch down bulky backpacks if needed).

Up top, continue following alongside the still-towering rocky formations to find the narrow opening at about 1.3 miles to a virtually hidden viewpoint with a blue metal viewing platform, which overlooks a more secluded portion of the canyon.

Left: "Holes in the Wall" near the entrance to Banshee Canyon.
Right: Climbing is easiest when gripping the rings with your hands and stepping on the ring mounts with your feet.

When ready, follow the service road past the water spigot and campground vault toilets (use these if the visitor center is closed) until you reach the visitor center and finish your loop back at the parking area.

MILES AND DIRECTIONS

0.0   Start at south trailhead, walking south.

0.1   Reach the first barbed-wire pass-through.

0.4   Arrive at the site of ancient petroglyphs.

0.8   Proceed through the second barbed-wire pass-through.

1.1   Come to the center of Banshee Canyon.

1.2   Ascend the climbing rings.

1.5   Finish at the parking area.

Note: While this trail could be hiked in reverse of this description, it's not recommended. In doing so you'd not only face the challenge of climbing down the ring loops rather than up, you'd essentially be giving your kids a three-layer chocolate cake for the first course and working backwards from there. Instead, be sure to start from the signed trailhead at the south end of the parking area, away from the visitors center, and hike in a clockwise direction.

27 HIDDEN VALLEY NATURE TRAIL

Step into a wonderous microclimate sheltered from the harsh Mojave Desert, where the pinyon-juniper woodland that covered the surrounding area more than 10,000 years ago can still be found. You'll follow a 1-mile loop trail with educational signs along the way and excellent bouldering opportunities for young children and grownups alike.

Start: West side of main parking area for Hidden Valley Picnic Area
Elevation gain: 100 feet
Distance: 1-mile loop
Difficulty: Easy to moderate (easy overall, but please note this trail has many stone steps without handrails and uneven surfaces, so it can present challenges for those of all ages who are not so steady on their feet)
Hiking time: 45 minutes to 1 hour
Ages on foot: 3 years+ (holding hands in some places)
Seasons/schedule: Oct through Apr
Fees: Weekly vehicle pass $$$$, annual National Parks pass, or Every Kid Outdoors Pass (*free* for fourth graders)
Trail contact: Joshua Tree National Park, 74485 National Park Dr.,
Twentynine Palms 92277, (760) 367-7511
Trail surface: Packed sand and rock
Land status: National park
Nearest town: Twentynine Palms
Dogs: No dogs
Toilets: At trailhead
Maps: Joshua Tree National Park map at www.nps.gov and the National Park App. Snap a photo of the detailed map of Hidden Valley Nature Trail posted at trailhead.
Special considerations: With no restaurants or concessions in Joshua Tree National Park, the Hidden Valley Picnic Area becomes especially busy during midday for visitors looking for a spot to stop and eat their lunches in addition to exploring this extremely popular trail. Avoid the thickest crowds by planning this hike early or late in the day.

FINDING THE TRAILHEAD

From the north, take CA 62 (Twentynine Palms Highway) and turn south onto Park Boulevard, continuing south and southeast 25 miles as this main route becomes briefly Quail Springs Road and then Park Boulevard once again. From the south at Cottonwood Visitor Center, take Pinto Basin Road north for 30 miles, then turn left (southwest) onto Park Boulevard. Continue west on Park Boulevard for 12 miles. At Intersection Rock, turn south at the entrance for Hidden Valley Picnic Area. Look for the information kiosk and well-marked trailhead with roped side rails leading you toward the first stone steps of the trail. **GPS:** N34 0.72' / W116 10.2'

THE HIKE

As you leave the busy parking lot of the Hidden Valley Picnic Area, it may be hard to imagine that in just 0.2 mile you'll feel you've entered a different world. After climbing the first set of steps, you'll pass through a narrow entrance, which was purportedly blasted open by resident rancher Bill Keys in 1936, just months before this land was declared a national monument. The native bunchgrass, which still grew in abundance in the sheltered valley, made it the ideal venue for pasturing his cattle.

Exploring the rocky wonderland within Joshua Tree's Hidden Valley.

As the trail splits, head left (west) to continue following the loop trail in a counter-clockwise direction. Sensitive people may feel the air change as they travel near the tall, rocky sides of the valley. Along here, rain runs down to collect in the granite-rich soil along the weathered rocks allowing plants normally seen only at higher elevations to continue thriving here as they did throughout these lower portions of the parkland thousands of years ago.

The high valley walls also shelter the adjacent soil and plants from the drying desert winds. Along this perimeter trail, you'll find bushy green pinyon pine trees, junipers, and even oaks growing close to the valley walls, while in the more exposed center, you'll see the familiar Joshua trees, blackbrush, and cacti found just outside the valley walls.

Bouldering enthusiasts may need (a lot of) extra time for this 1-mile hike.

A feathery pinyon pine thrives beside a sheltering, rain-collecting rock wall.

The feathery, single-needle pinyons were an important resource for the native people who lived in this area. The Serrano people (who called themselves Yuhaviatam, or "people of the pines") were the main group living in this portion of today's Joshua Tree National Park and are thought to have arrived in this part of California some 2,500 years ago. Not only could they use the wood from pinyon pines for fire and construction, but the pitch was invaluable for waterproofing their baskets and patching broken pottery. Better still, they could collect the green cones and roast them in a fire until they "popped open," revealing freshly roasted pine seeds that provided excellent nutrition.

As you continue around the main trail, learning more about the flora, fauna, and geology of this little valley from the interpretive signs, you'll notice side trails taking off to and through some enticing boulders. For some young visitors, climbing around on *these*

Fun (and funny) photo ops await along
Hidden Valley Nature Trail.

may be the most memorable part of the hike. Just be sure not to lose sight of each other during your explorations. Without view of the parking area or entrance to the valley, it can be easy to lose your sense of direction here—or lose sight of a small person behind some large boulders.

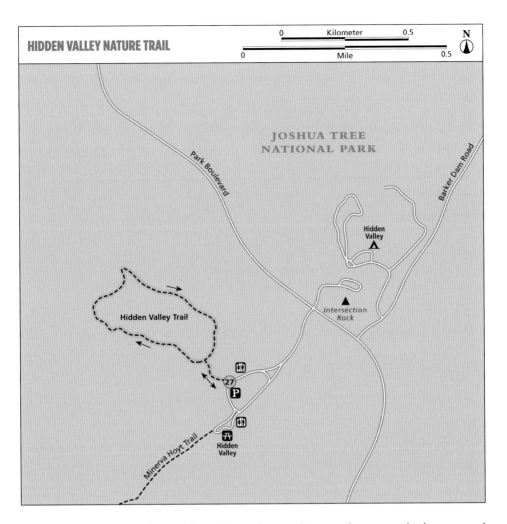

JOSHUA TREE NATIONAL PARK

Park Boulevard

Barker Dam Road

Hidden Valley

Hidden Valley Trail

Intersection Rock

27

P

Hidden Valley

Minerva Hoyt Trail

If you lose your place on the perimeter loop trail, just work your way back out toward the valley's rock walls and pick up the trail where you find it, watching for the next informational sign along the way. Continue your clockwise exploration until you return to the signed turnoff and follow your steps back to the picnic area.

MILES AND DIRECTIONS

0.0 Start at the marked trailhead and information kiosk.

0.1 Turn left (west) onto the perimeter loop trail; continue following trail and signs clockwise.

0.9 Turn left (south) to follow the trail back to parking and the picnic area.

1.0 Arrive back at the trailhead.

28 ARCH ROCK

Though nowhere near the grandiose scale of those you'll see in Arches National Park, Joshua Tree's Arch Rock still makes for a fun, family hiking destination and photo opportunity. For bouldering enthusiasts big and small, there's also a fantastic natural playground to explore near the arch with easy climbing opportunities.

Start: Twin Tanks parking area
Elevation gain: 88 feet
Distance: 1.4-mile lollipop
Difficulty: Easy to moderate depending on how much bouldering you want to do
Hiking time: About 35 minutes or more depending on how much time you want to explore the boulders in this area
Ages on foot: 3 years+
Seasons/schedule: Oct through Apr
Fees and permits: Weekly vehicle pass $$$$, annual National Parks pass, or Every Kid Outdoors Pass (*free* for fourth graders)
Trail contact: Joshua Tree National Park, 74485 National Park Dr.,

Twentynine Palms 92277, (760) 367-7511
Trail surface: Dirt with some gravel, then boulders if you want a good look at the arch or additional easy bouldering
Land status: National park
Nearest town: Twentynine Palms
Dogs: No dogs
Toilets: None
Maps: Joshua Tree National Park map at www.nps.gov and the National Park App
Special considerations: Heat and wildlife; use caution when climbing boulders

FINDING THE TRAILHEAD

From the north, take CA 62 (Twentynine Palms Highway) and turn south onto Utah Trail, where you can make a quick stop at the Oasis Visitor Center before continuing south as Utah Trail becomes Park Boulevard. At 8.6 miles (from CA 62), you'll take the left fork (south) onto Pinto Basin Road in the direction of the Cottonwood Visitor Center. In 2.2 miles, you'll turn right (south) into the Twin Tanks parking area. The trailhead is at the south end of the parking area. **GPS:** N33 59.3' / W116 2.25'

THE HIKE

Although this is one of the most-hiked trails in Joshua Tree National Park, with one of the most-photographed landmarks within the park, you might be surprised how unobvious it is to find and stay on the right trail.

First of all, parking for this popular trail is now at the "Twin Tanks/Arch Rock Nature Trail parking area" (the geographically closer White Tank Campground parking is now reserved for campers only). You'll proceed out the south end of the parking area past the sign with arrows pointing straight for both the "California Riding and Hiking Trail" and "Arch Rock Nature Trail." Just beyond the sign and short wooden fence rails, you'll see the registration board for backcountry camping and a large map of the area on display. You might want to take a phone photo of the area map for backup.

Continue on the dirt trail to where a second set of wooden fence rails forms a three-way split, with a sign labeled "California Riding and Hiking Trail" at the top and an arrow indicating that Arch Rock Trail is 0.2 miles to your left (southeast). Pay close

The Rivoli sisters getting their snapshot beneath Arch Rock.

attention as you're actually 0.2 mile from where you started back at the trailhead, and you're almost to the trail turnoff already.

From here you will carefully cross Pinto Basin Road to where the well-marked trail continues forward through another guiding set of welcoming fence rails. But while your instincts might suggest the dominant path continuing straight would head toward the popular arch, you will instead take an immediate right (southeast) just *before* the wooden fencing onto a much less-notable dirt trail. Look closely to your right and you'll see a small sign with an arrow labeled "Arch Rock."

Given the short distance of this hike and the acres of wide-open desert around you, you might find yourself wondering at this point why you can't see the slightest hint of the geologic wonder you seek. Fear not. You are, at least for the moment, still on the right trail.

Continue another 0.4 mile on the relatively flat dirt path through occasional Joshua trees and infrequent boulders increasing in size, ignoring faint suggestions of sidetrack paths that might put independent young hikers too close to cacti for comfort. Instead, keep an eye out for the minimalist posts with index card–sized brown arrows pointing to the sky to continue leading you in the right direction (aka straight).

When the path splits, head to your right (south), but bear left in 0.1 mile to avoid an unnecessary visit to the White Tank Campground (unless you need a restroom) and continue toward Arch Rock.

If you find yourself wondering, yet again, why you still can't detect the slightest hint of the geologic wonder you seek as your final 0.25 mile ticks by, take heart. As the ancient rocks loom higher around you, you'll likely see increasing numbers of hikers climbing up the large boulders to seize a photo op, to take a rest, or to scratch their heads and wonder aloud, "But where is the arch?" Watch carefully for an unassuming, little brown sign toward your right (south), which, when you get close enough, you'll see reads "The Arch."

Step closer to this sign and you'll see the stone head of an elephant appear before you (or perhaps Snuffleupagus) with its trunk extending in a graceful arch pointing away from you. Congratulations, my friends, you've found Arch Rock. To reach the arch itself,

Top left: The moment the arch at last comes into view—like an elephant feeding itself rocks. (Just ask your kids if they can see it, too!)
Top right: The flat, easy terrain en route to Arch Rock.
Bottom: Delightful distractions? You'll find all kinds of easy bouldering opportunities as you get closer to Arch Rock.

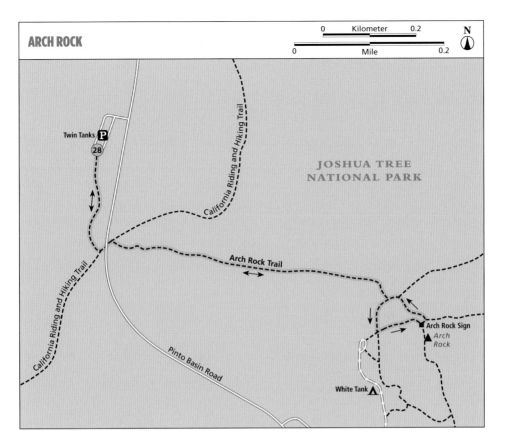

you'll need to climb up the sloping rock face toward it, possibly waiting as other hikers take their turns.

Friendly Tip: To get the best photos of the arch (or your family standing with it), you'll want to scramble up the side of the boulders narrowly across from the arch.

While most trail maps show this as a clearly defined lollipop, you'll see undefined paths crisscrossing throughout the loop area, most leading to and around the best climbing boulders. Explore to your hearts' content before retracing the same route back to your car.

MILES AND DIRECTIONS

0.0   Start at the trailhead.

0.2   Turn left onto California Riding and Hiking Trail and cross Pinto Basin Road, then take an immediate right onto Arch Rock Trail.

0.5   Turn right onto the lollipop.

0.6   Bear left at the fork (east).

0.7   Arrive at the small "Arch Rock" sign; proceed past the sign to the hidden Arch. When ready, continue around the lollipop (northwest) and double back on Arch Rock Trail.

1.4   Return to the trailhead and parking area.

29 CHOLLA CACTUS GARDEN NATURE TRAIL

For many, Joshua Tree National Park conjures images of gargantuan boulders and its namesake trees. But this easy walk (and great stop for stretching little legs) opens your eyes to an entirely different side of the park—the Pinto Basin. Here a sprawling stand of captivating "teddy bear cacti" (aka Bigelow cholla) welcome visitors with a wide and well-marked path.

Start: The well-marked trail begins at the sign at the southwest end of the parking lot.
Elevation gain: 10 feet
Distance: 0.25-mile loop
Difficulty: Easy
Hiking time: About 15 minutes
Ages on foot: 3 years+
Seasons/schedule: Best Oct through Apr
Fees: Weekly vehicle pass $$$$, annual National Parks pass, or Every Kid Outdoors Pass (*free* for fourth graders)
Trail contact: Joshua Tree National Park, 74485 National Park Dr., Twentynine Palms 92277, (760) 367-7511

Trail surface: Packed sand and wooden boardwalk
Land status: National park
Nearest town: Twentynine Palms
Dogs: No dogs
Toilets: None
Maps: Joshua Tree National Park map at www.nps.gov and the National Park App
Special considerations: Prickly cacti! Make sure your child knows, as fuzzy as they may look, these "teddy bear cacti" are not to be touched.
Gear suggestions: Children too young to understand not to touch the cacti should be carried or pushed in a stroller (stroller-friendly trail).

FINDING THE TRAILHEAD

If entering the park from the south via I-10, you'll take exit 168 for Cottonwood Springs Road and proceed north on Cottonwood Springs Road for 6.9 miles. At Cottonwood Visitor Center, you can stop off to purchase your park pass, get your park map and Junior Ranger booklet, and use the restrooms (recommended as there aren't many in this part of the park). From here, Cottonwood Road becomes Pinto Basin Road, which you will follow northeast another 19.8 miles until the Cholla Cactus Garden comes into view, with parking to your left (southwest). **GPS:** N33 55.52' / W115 55.73'

If entering the park from the north, take CA 62 (Twentynine Palms Highway) and turn south onto Utah Trail, where you can make a quick stop at the Oasis Visitor Center before continuing south as Utah Trail becomes Park Boulevard. At 8.6 miles (from CA 62), you'll take the left fork (south) onto Pinto Basin Road in the direction of the Cottonwood Visitor Center. In 10 miles you'll turn right (south) into the parking area for the Cholla Cactus Garden.

THE HIKE

Though it's not much farther than Joshua Tree's most popular (and often congested) destinations (only 12 minutes' drive from Arch Rock Nature Trail), the Cholla Cactus Garden Nature Trail shows visitors an entirely different side of this vast park.

Some Bigelow cholla, aka Teddy Bear cacti, have grown up to 8 feet tall in the garden.

In the absence of Joshua trees and gigantic geologic formations, this nature trail offers sweeping views over the Pinto Basin, where the Mojave and Sonoran Deserts meet, hemmed in by the Pinto, Coxcomb, and Eagle Mountains (to the west and north, east, and south, respectively). Competing for your immediate attention, however, will be the fuzzy army of Bigelow cholla standing from Ewok height up to 8 feet tall in some places.

As soon as you start down the signed trail at the southwest end of the parking lot, you'll quickly understand how they earned the nickname Teddy Bear Cholla or Teddy Bear

Top: Enjoy beautiful views of the Pinto Basin from the Cholla Cactus Garden.
Bottom: The packed sand and boardwalk nature trail is stroller friendly.

Cactus. With their furry jointed arms and legs, they often give the appearance of stuffed animals on sticks. Make sure your child knows they're as prickly and painful to the touch as any other cactus would be (for children too small to understand, carriers or strollers may be best here).

Follow the relatively flat path in a counterclockwise direction as it winds through the cholla over stretches of packed sand and boardwalk. Between March and May, you may have the added pleasure of seeing these cholla in bloom with their pale-yellow blossoms. Other desert plants can also be seen blooming here from February through late May, including beavertail and hedgehog cacti, desert senna, white ratany, and desert lavender

0   Kilometer   0.25

0   Mile   0.25

N

× 2,508 ft., 765 m

JOSHUA TREE WILDERNESS

JOSHUA TREE NATIONAL PARK

To Twentynine Palms, 62

2,320 ft., 707 m ×

29

Cholla Cactus Garden Nature Trail

Cholla Cactus Garden

Pinto Basin Road

To 10

P I N T O   B A S I N

OH, RATS!

Desert woodrats love Teddy Bear Cholla, too! As you stroll this nature trail, look for piled up sections of old cactus that help protect their nests hidden underneath from coyotes and other predators.

Teddy bears on sticks? The jointed, furry branches of these cholla look like stuffed animals.

among others. An overview of all these desert bloomers can be seen in the Joshua Tree National Park Botanical Trail Guide for the garden available online at www.nps.gov/jotr/learn/nature/cholla-cactus-garden.htm.

After a 0.25-mile stroll over packed sand and sections of boardwalk, the loop path returns you to the trailhead and parking area.

Friendly Tip: The Cholla Cactus Garden Nature Trail is most photogenic and pleasant in the early morning or evening when the sun is low enough to shine through the cacti's hairy exteriors, setting them aglow.

You may or may not find a printed interpretive guide for a fee at the trail's entrance on your visit—though fret not if the supply is out, as you don't need the guide to enjoy your visit to the garden.

MILES AND DIRECTIONS

0.0   Start at the signed trailhead and follow the path counterclockwise.

0.25   Return to the trailhead, loop complete.

30 LADDER CANYON AND PAINTED CANYON

This bucket-list family adventure in the Mecca Hills Wilderness is not for the faint of heart. You'll wend your way through a narrow, winding slot canyon with aluminum ladders up to 12 feet tall (which may or may not have all their rungs and should not be presumed to be attached to anything) leading you up and down a series of dry falls with some scrambling required. Then continue your ascent up to a spectacular ridge view toward Coachella Valley—and keep on climbing up to a 360-degree panoramic vista. After a sudden, steep descent down a straight-shot, dirt singletrack, you'll return through colorful Painted Canyon with two more ladders down for good measure.

Start: Painted Canyon Trailhead
Elevation gain: 856 feet
Distance: 4.4-mile loop
Difficulty: Strenuous (even in the nontechnical areas, deep sand gives an extra workout)
Hiking time: 3 to 4 hours
Seasons/schedule: Oct through Apr, only when conditions are dry
Ages on foot: 7 years+
Fees: None
Trail contact: Bureau of Land Management, Palm Springs South Coast Field Office, 1201 Bird Center Dr., Palm Springs 92262, (760) 833-7100, BLM_CA_Web_PS@blm.gov
Trail surface: Sand, rock
Land status: Public
Nearest town: Mecca
Dogs: While dogs are technically allowed off leash under voice command on these trails (BLM land), most dogs cannot climb up or down steep, aluminum ladders, so this hike is not recommended for our four-legged friends.
Toilets: Not here, but you will see pit toilets at a different staging area on your left as you drive in, approximately 1 mile before the Painted Canyon trailhead

Maps: Take a photo of the BLM map showing these trails posted in the information kiosk at the trailhead (or better yet, bring a photo of this map)
Special considerations: Technical points in the hike include ladders, some with tricky transitions to the levels above, some slippery (worn smooth) and uneven rock surfaces, and a steep descent in loose dirt into Painted Canyon. Heat and sun exposure can be intense by late morning, so start early when temperatures are lower, and you'll still have some shade along the canyon wall upon your return. Also, be mindful of rattlesnakes, which do make appearances here.
Gear suggestions: Magnetic compass and physical map strongly recommended. If hiking with infants and babies, know that baby backpack carriers and front packs for toddlers won't fit through some of the narrow ladder chutes and canyon passages, so this hike is recommended only for kids who can do the climbing and hiking on their own.

FINDING THE TRAILHEAD

From CA 111 / Grapefruit Boulevard, exit northeast at 4th Street for Mecca. Take the first right (southeast) onto Hammond Road, and in 0.2 mile turn left (east) onto 66th Avenue (not to be confused with 66th Avenue on the west side of the highway, which is not connected). Continue east for 3.9 miles to where

66th Avenue becomes Box Canyon Road, then drive another 1 mile. Just after the backward S curve, turn left (northwest) onto the dirt Painted Canyon Road. Proceed 4.7 miles on this delightfully bumpy (washboard) road, taking care not to slow or stop in any areas of loose, deep dirt (please see my friendly tip that follows). At the end of the road, you'll see the parking area (also dirt/sand). The trailhead is by the wooden information kiosk with map at the east end of the parking area (not to be confused with a different trail that leaves from the west). The correct trail will lead you northeast into Painted Canyon. **GPS:** N33 37.15' / W115 59.94'

Note: While a road sign advises four-wheel-drive only on Painted Canyon Road, the road is generally well maintained in dry seasons with plenty of non-four-wheel-drive cars making the journey each year (though understand you will be doing so at your own risk). It's recommended to call the BLM office at the number above to check the status of the road (and these trails) before you head out.

THE HIKE

As you enter the sandy wash of Painted Canyon, with its magnificent sandstone walls rising high beside you, ignore the immediate offshoot to your left (at 0.1 mile), which becomes the Ropes Canyon trail (see note), and instead proceed 0.4 mile farther into Painted Canyon.

An easily missed trail marker appears on the right side (east) of the canyon, pointing left (west) across the canyon for no obvious reason. There may or may not also be arrows (created from rocks) in the sand pointing you left toward some large boulders beside the canyon wall. Look closer and step between these boulders to find the first ladder leading you up a dry waterfall chute into Ladder Canyon. (Long ago, there was a Ladder Canyon sign here, which has since disappeared.)

Continue along the narrow slot canyon, with a second ladder leading you down, then nearly vertical third and fourth ladders leading you up and up again as you make your way through the narrow, tightly winding maze of deep, dark canyon passages. Be aware that you're not only likely to lose GPS signal here, but your sense of direction and distance may be compromised as well. With all the small steps and turning and near-vertical ladders, an analog pedometer may show you've covered twice the distance when you finish this section.

At last, the canyon opens wider and the trail continues to ascend. At 0.8 mile (which might feel more like 2 miles), you'll see an established trail take off to your left (northwest) with possibly a rock cairn marking the intersection. Stay to the right (northeast vs. northwest), where you'll soon have the opportunity to test your inner bighorn sheep (and if you're lucky, you might even see one).

As you leave Ladder Canyon behind, the trail turns to mostly gravel and rocks. Elegant ocotillo and scrubby desert brush appear as the rugged, rocky incline grows so steep it appears to be topped only by sky. Keep climbing. At the top you'll discover a glorious vista from the ridge—the first of the hike and best for photos. Take a water break and enjoy the views over the chocolate- and caramel-colored hills with a glimpse of the Salton Sea in the distance.

Note: Spur trails venture out to scenic "selfie" spots here, but don't mistake them for your actual trail. (Trail stewards have placed solid lines of rocks across the trail leading southeast advising hikers not to continue.) Instead, you'll continue north from this ridge in the direction of the radio towers you'll see atop a neighboring ridge.

Climbing up a dry waterfall in Ladder Canyon.

Top: The return hike through Painted Canyon.
Bottom: The Rivoli kids pause for a photo on a ridge high between Ladder and Painted Canyons.

This exposed, gravelly stretch will give you occasional glimpses into Painted Canyon far below as you continue the final (and perhaps thirstiest) part of your climb. At 2 miles, you'll reach the highest point of this hike, marked by a few dozen rock cairns stacked at the peak. Be sure to stop and enjoy the 360-degree view over Coachella Valley and the Mecca Hills.

Climbing down one of the final ladders of the hike in Painted Canyon.

From here the trail heads east, descending rapidly toward Painted Canyon. However, when you glimpse the canyon floor still so far below, you may wonder just how your family will get down there so quickly. That's about when the trail before you appears to drop off a cliff.

As you carefully approach the precipice, you'll see an extremely steep, narrow dirt trail slanting down against the hillside toward the bottom of Painted Canyon (another chance to test your inner bighorn sheep). Proceed with care, slow and steady, and don't be afraid to scoot on your backsides.

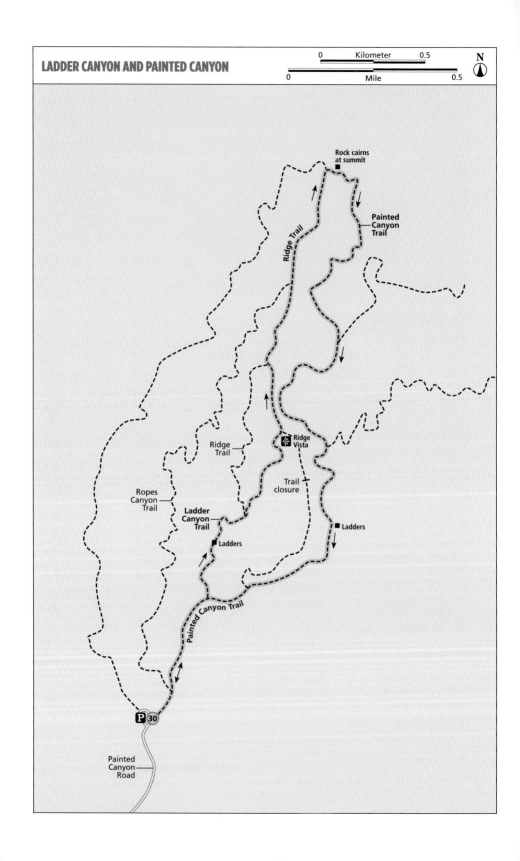

0 Kilometer 0.5

0 Mile 0.5

N

Rock cairns at summit

Painted Canyon Trail

Ridge Trail

Ridge Vista

Ridge Trail

Trail closure

Ropes Canyon Trail

Ladders

Ladder Canyon Trail

Ladders

Painted Canyon Trail

P 30

Painted Canyon Road

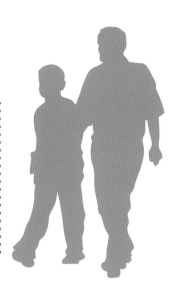

TREASURES IN THE DESERT?

Painted Canyon is not just a "hidden gem"—it's also filled with hidden gems! As you hike back through upper Painted Canyon, watch for striations of rose, brown, and purple quartz in the canyon walls and keep an eye out for small crystalline treasures scattered throughout the sandy canyon floor.

Once you reach the wash of upper Painted Canyon, you may have the opportunity to enjoy shade once again, whether from occasional smoke trees or the canyon walls themselves (midday you will have the least shade through this final stretch, so plan accordingly). Though the hiking is relatively level and gently downward sloping, the deep sand adds an extra dimension of rigor. Be sure to take water and snack breaks accordingly.

At 3.3 miles, you'll arrive at the final two ladders of your adventure, leading you down a pair of dry falls. Continue on down the canyon trail and before you know it you'll be passing the hidden entrance to Ladder Canyon. Retrace your steps to the trailhead where the whole adventure began, and hopefully to some extra water awaiting in your car.

MILES AND DIRECTIONS

0.0   Start at Painted Canyon Trailhead.

0.4   Ladder Canyon Trail begins with the first ladder at the left side of trail, concealed by boulders.

0.8   Stay right (north) at the fork.

1.1   Arrive at the first ridge with views; continue straight (north) toward radio towers.

2.0   Arrive at the peak with panoramic views and marked with rock cairns.

3.3   Reach the final pair of ladders, which will lead you down.

4.4   Return to trailhead.

Side Trip: If you're curious about Ropes Canyon, it's advisable to save it for the end of this hike to see if your family still has the energy for it (and water). Also, understand the ropes are not regularly inspected or guaranteed to be safe, so you'll be using them at your own risk.

31 BORREGO PALM CANYON

Hike to a peaceful stream and follow it up through a narrowing canyon to a desert oasis with a grove of towering California fan palms, the only palms native to the western United States. Though the palm grove suffered a horrendous, human-caused fire in 2020, thankfully the trees survived, and visitors can hike the trail to view them as the grove recovers and the oasis is restored. Also, keep an eye out for bighorn sheep along the way!

Start: Signed trailhead at west edge of parking area
Elevation gain: 344 feet (or 700 feet with alternate route)
Distance: 3-mile out-and-back, or alternate 3-mile lollipop
Difficulty: Moderate to strenuous due to many rocky steps and large rocks themselves to step up and down with some scrambling along the way. Heat is often an added challenge. The "Alternate" return route has an additional 350 feet elevation gain as noted.
Hiking time: About 2 hours+
Ages on foot: 4 years+
Seasons/schedule: Late fall through spring, not advisable in summer
Fees: $$ day-use fee, California Explorer Pass, or 4th graders free with the California Adventure Pass
Trail contact: Anza-Borrego Desert State Park Headquarters, 200 Palm Canyon Dr., Borrego Springs 92004,

(760) 767-4205; Anza-Borrego Desert State Park Wildflower Hotline (760) 767-4684
Trail surface: Dirt and rock
Land status: State park
Nearest town: Borrego Springs
Other trail users: None
Water availability: At restrooms
Dogs: No dogs on trail
Toilets: At parking area and in adjacent campground
Maps: USGS Borrego Palm Canyon and official park map
Special considerations: Heat and exposure with possible rattlesnakes and scorpions, so stay on trail and stay together. Park rangers advise bringing 1 gallon of water per person for this hike and avoiding it entirely in summer months.
Gear suggestions: For those who appreciate trekking poles, you'll be glad to have them here.

FINDING THE TRAILHEAD

From Christmas Circle in central Borrego Springs, take the exit west for Palm Canyon Drive and continue straight for 1.6 miles before either A) continuing straight to stop at the visitors center first, or B) turning right (north) onto the unnamed service road leading to the Borrego Palm Canyon Campground in 1 mile. Continue through the campground area until the road ends at the parking area for the Borrego Palm Canyon trail. You'll find the signed Palm Canyon trailhead at the west edge of the parking area. **GPS:** N33 16.2' / W116 25.08'

THE HIKE

Before your hike, download the Nature Trail Guide for "Palm Canyon Trail" from the California State Parks website section on hiking in Anza-Borrego (www.parks.ca.gov). This family-friendly guide gives an overview of fifteen things to look for as you hike this trail, with interesting details about the desert plants, animals, insects, and signs of the early Cahuilla Indian ancestors who called this canyon home.

Borrego Palm Canyon greets hikers with blossoming golden brittlebush in spring.

Start at the "Palm Grove 1.5 mile" trail sign at the west edge of the parking lot, heading down the rock-lined dirt path with some of the smaller Santa Rosa Mountains directly in front of you.

In late winter or early spring, you may find yourself surrounded by golden mounds of blossoming brittlebush, desert lavender, or beavertail cactus blooming alongside several other species of desert wildflowers here—especially on a "superbloom" year (call the wildflower hotline listed above for updates).

Palm Canyon Creek on a visit with significant water flow.

At 0.1 mile you'll stay right at the signed fork, continuing on the now "Palm Oasis" trail. The other fork, marked "Alternate," will be your return route if you opt for it. From here, your route becomes more characteristic of a canyon wash, with the possibility of creek crossings starting at 0.3 mile, though the water flow here varies dramatically from one year to the next. On the driest years, you might not see water until much farther up the trail—or possibly not at all.

Often, there is a calm stream flowing through here, fed by the springs beneath the palm oasis. However, with rare but intense rain can come rare but intense flooding (most often in late summer). Imagine the runoff from 22 square miles of area, including San Diego County's highest point at Hot Springs Mountain (6,407 feet), draining into this canyon during a summer storm.

The most notable flooding of the century so far took place in 2004, when rains brought mud and debris from far and wide to the canyon floor. Take a close look at the "logs" lining parts of the trail. They're actually the trunks of tall palm trees deposited here in that storm.

As the canyon narrows, you'll notice the rocks and boulders increasing in size. These, too, were carried to the canyon floor by flash-flooding events over time. But on dry hiking days, they can add a whole new element of fun for kid explorers, with bouldering opportunities and small cave-like niches to explore along the way (just check for critters first!).

If you have the good fortune to visit while there is adequate waterflow in the wash, you may soon hear—and quickly see a small waterfall flowing over a large boulder around 1 mile (a rare desert delight). The canyon vegetation increases along this stretch

The Rivoli kids at the Palm Oasis before the fire.

as well, providing a lush sense of relief in the dry desert heat. Watch for the tallest of the palms to suddenly appear in the distance.

At last you'll step out from a narrow slot between boulders to view the Palm Oasis itself. Be sure to respect the boundaries set for viewing the grove as it recovers. Though burnt to what looked like tall black toothpicks in early 2020, these resilient California fan palms have since regenerated new green crowns and are working on replacement "grass

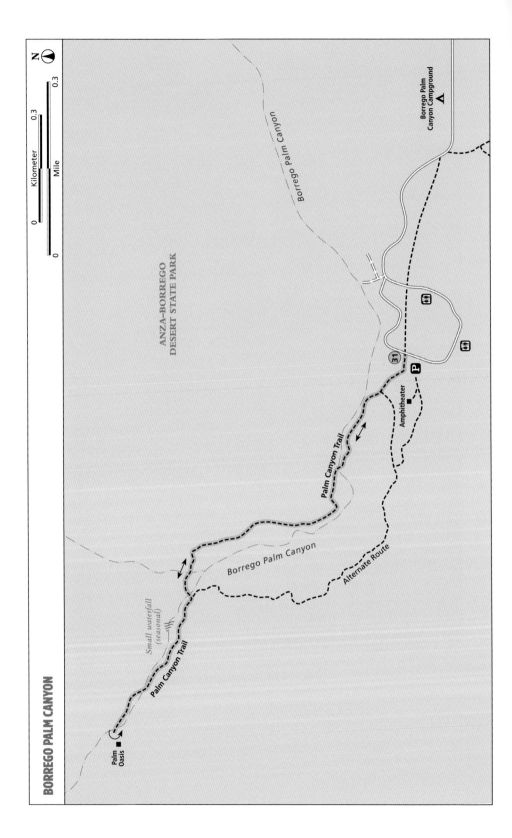

BORREGO PALM CANYON

N

Kilometer
0   0.3

Mile
0   0.3

ANZA–BORREGO
DESERT STATE PARK

Borrego Palm Canyon

Palm
Oasis

Palm Canyon Trail

Small waterfall
(seasonal)

Borrego Palm Canyon

Palm Canyon Trail

Alternate Route

Amphitheater

31

P

Borrego Palm
Canyon Campground

skirts," the shaggy buildup of old fronds characteristic of these trees, which help guard them against insects and provide habitat for small wildlife.

Enjoy a picnic or well-earned snack and water break atop the boulders here before retracing your steps to the trailhead.

MILES AND DIRECTIONS

0.0	Start at the trailhead.
0.1	Stay right (northeast) at the signed fork for Palm Canyon.
1.0	Alternate trail rejoins the route; continue straight (north).
1.1	Arrive at the site of a possible small waterfall (seasonal).
1.5	Arrive at Palm Oasis; reverse course when ready (taking signed "Alternate" route if desired).
3.0	Return to trailhead.

Option: While most kids will likely prefer the variety and lesser elevation gain of the Palm Canyon Trail for the return hike, the higher and drier Alternate Route is an option. Just remember, if you opt for this route, you'll be nowhere near the stream and will have an additional 350 feet of elevation gain still to go before rejoining the trail and returning to the same trailhead.

THE DAILY GRIND

Cahuilla women who lived in this canyon area long ago ground seeds in the same places on some rocks over many generations. This helped create the holes or *morteros* you might see for yourself if you look closely at the rocky surfaces along the trail. If you see one, look also for signs of their grinding slicks or *metates*, which may have been used to smash the seeds.

Watch for *morteros* worn in the rocks by generations of the Cahuilla People as you hike.

32 **BAT CAVES BUTTES**

This desert hike takes you from below sea level to the strange formation of Bat Caves Buttes, once an island in an ancient lake that filled this area. Look for fossils, rose quartz, and lightning glass along the way, and bring your flashlight—you may have the chance to see Townsend's Big Eared bats snoozing in the caves. As you return, enjoy views of the Salton Sea and the San Jacinto Mountains in the distance.

Start: On the elevated dirt road running parallel to the train tracks (opposite the parking area)

Elevation gain: 225 feet, more if bouldering at the caves

Distance: 2.4-mile out-and-back or more depending on how much bouldering and extra exploration you want to do at the caves

Difficulty: Moderate to strenuous because walking in the loose, deep soil is a workout in itself and there is the opportunity for scrambling up rocks if desired

Hiking time: About 1.5 hours

Ages on foot: 7 years+

Seasons/schedule: Oct through Apr

Fees: Free

Trail contact: Salton Sea State Recreation Area, 100-225 State Park Rd., North Shore 92254, (760) 393-3059 or (760) 393-3810, www.parks .ca.gov

Trail surface: Loose, powdery dirt and rocks

Land status: State recreation area

Nearest town: Niland

Dogs: Yes, off leash, but be on the alert for rattlesnakes and ATV activity

Toilets: None

Maps: USGS quadrangle map for Durmid

Other trail users: ATVs

Special considerations: Rattlesnakes are present in this area. As always, any kids scrambling on the rocks should be watchful for wildlife and careful of where they put their hands. ATVs also use this area.

Gear suggestions: Flashlights or head lamps to help see bats if present.

FINDING THE TRAILHEAD

 From Niland, drive northwest on CA 111 / Grapefruit Boulevard. Start watching your odometer at Bombay Beach, and in 8 miles turn right (east) into the packed dirt parking area marked only by an Adopt-a-Highway sign. From Mecca, drive southeast on CA 111 / Grapefruit Boulevard roughly 19 miles and watch for the Imperial County Line sign opposite the parking area. Ignore any outdated information that says to look for an abandoned diner here—you won't find one. Once parked, walk to the Southern Pacific Railroad tracks; the elevated line passes at the east edge of the parking area and is visible for miles in both directions. Take a good look in each direction. When you're certain it's safe, climb up and over the tracks. You'll descend on the other side of the tracks, then climb back up onto the raised dirt road running parallel to the tracks. **GPS:** N33 25.61' / W115 49.85'

THE HIKE

Staring up at the foreboding elevated railroad track with its rocky slope and no trace of a trail in sight, you can take pride in the knowledge that this family hike is not for the timid. (Of course, with a description like "bat caves" and the spartan desert locale, you might have guessed that already.)

The Rivoli kids strike a pose at Bat Caves Buttes near the Salton Sea.

Take a good look in both directions to make sure there isn't a train in sight, then clamber up and over the railroad tracks (east) in the direction of the easily identified buttes in the distance. On the other side, you'll find an elevated dirt road running parallel to the tracks along here. Walk up onto the dirt road and head south/southeast for about 0.25 mile.

Here you'll descend to the desert floor, where an informal dirt road makes its way northeast through puffs of creosote bushes toward Bat Caves Buttes, curving slightly here

View from a cave toward the Salton Sea and San Jacinto Mountains.

and there for interest with a bright yellow pipeline marker visible at 0.5 mile to help you know you're on the right track. Where any informal ATV routes may cross (changeable by the season and year), just continue straight on the main course toward the tallest of the buttes.

Most of this desert hike takes place *below* sea level. This "faulty" geological area, known as the Salton Sink, is actually a landlocked extension of the Gulf of California, separating Baja California from mainland Mexico. Over thousands of years, the basin saw many cycles of filling and draining as the Colorado River changed courses between the Rocky Mountains and the gulf. At times, the gulf water also flowed inland, adding salt water and silt deposits to the fresh river water in the Salton Sink.

However, an accident in 1905 created the Salton Sea as we know it today. When the Colorado River escaped an irrigation canal, it began filling (and filling!) the Salton Sink for 16 months straight. Entire communities were lost to the flooding, including the city of Salton and part of the Torres Martinez Reservation of Desert Cahuilla Indians. And the main line of the Southern Pacific Railroad, which had run along this side of the lake, was also submerged (now you know why the replacement tracks you crossed over are elevated—just in case).

Today, the Salton Sea sits at 235 feet below sea level, and at 35 miles long and 15 miles wide, it's the largest lake in California—and by far the saltiest! With no outlet for any of the water and minerals that collect in it and continual evaporation, today's Salton Sea is 50 percent saltier than the ocean. Only tough-as-nails tilapia and the hearty desert pupfish are known to still successfully reproduce in this water.

As you gain elevation, progressing toward the buttes, the views behind you over the strangely beautiful sea steadily improve. But don't forget to watch where you step, too. In the sand, you may see bits of rose quartz, travertine, calcite, lightning glass, or fossils.

As the buttes come more clearly into view, note their striped strata thrust upward by the San Andreas fault. You'll

Watch for rose quartz, travertine, lightning glass, and fossils along the way—though probably not fossilized dinosaur eggs. (Though one can always hope.)

begin to see the mouths of the caves that formed as the weaker layers of strata weathered away. Evidence of past water lines suggest that, at least once in its geologic history, this butte may have been an island. Lake Cahuilla, the most recent of the freshwater lakes that filled the sink, was six times the size of the present Salton Sea. The lapping of its lake water likely contributed to the erosion and formation of the most angular of these cave openings, while sandblasting wind most likely shaped the more rounded of the openings.

MY, WHAT BIG EARS YOU HAVE!

Just how big are the ears of a Townsend's big-eared bat? For a full-size adult bat, the ears may be 1.5 inches long—about half the length of its body! When these bats sleep, their ears curl up snug and tight, looking much like the horns of a ram.

Exiting a narrow cave at the northeast end of Bat Caves Buttes.

If you've timed your visit early enough in the day, you will enjoy plentiful shade along the cave side of the buttes. The largest caves greet you first at the right (southeast) end of the buttes, though you may have better luck finding the Townsend's big-eared bats that live here in the smaller, less-visited caves to the northwest. With only 3-inch-long bodies, tucked tightly as they snooze by day, they can be difficult to spot, especially since they can look like dusty dried leaves or bumps on a rocky surface. If you're having trouble spotting any, step inside of the narrow cave to the northeast with entrances on two sides and stay very, very quiet. You might hear a nursery of bats deep in the recesses or through a cavern wall.

As you pass the final ground-level cave at the northwest end of the buttes, turn back to face the largest caves and give a loud clap. When you determine the right place to

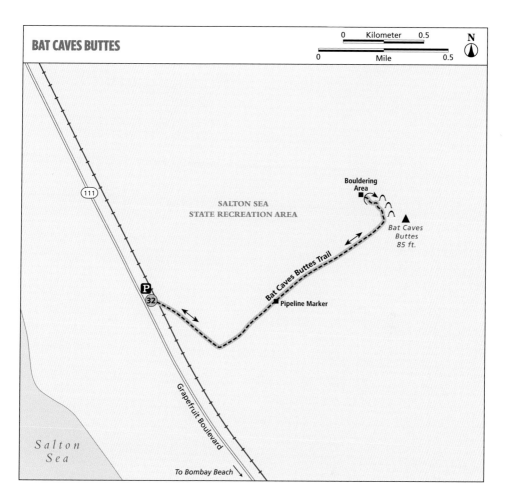

stand, you'll have a perfect echo. From here, you may want to scramble up the boulders and rocks that continue above with some additional small caves (proceed with care in case of wildlife).

When ready, retrace your steps back to the parking area where you began.

MILES AND DIRECTIONS

0.0   Start on the elevated dirt ATV road after crossing the railroad tracks; head to your right (southeast).

0.3   Walk down from the dirt road to the dirt trail heading northeast toward the buttes.

0.5   Pass by the yellow petroleum pipeline marker.

1.0   Arrive at the first of the caves and farthest to the right (southeast); work your way in and out of caves progressing leftward (northwest).

1.2   Reach the end of the ground-level caves. (**Option:** Venture up the boulders for more adventure.) Reverse your steps back to the parking area.

2.4   Return to the parking area.

A small, bonus waterfall on the return hike from Paradise Falls.

LOS ANGELES AND SURROUNDING AREA

You can check any prior notions of LA being one long freeway at the first trailhead. Just an exit away from I-5 (and a stone's throw from Warner Brothers Studios), you'll find the sprawling 4,210-acre Griffith Park with its 53-mile network of hiking trails—the largest municipal park with urban wilderness in the United States.

Just a short drive from there, you'll enter the Santa Monica National Recreation Area, celebrated as the *world's* largest urban national park, with 153,075 acres of open space and more than 500 miles of trails for hikers to explore.

Nearly half of Los Angeles County is, in fact, mountainous. Its network of east-west ranges, which run from the Santa Monica Mountains hugging the Pacific in the west through the San Bernardino Mountains rising steeply in the east, are the product of tectonic forces along the San Andreas fault.

Throughout the area, you'll find family-friendly trails leading you to wildflower-filled hillsides and meadows, through mixed-pine forests and mountain trails, and to hidden waterfalls. Here are five favorites to get you started.

33 **PARADISE FALLS**

Descend into a deep, prickly-pear–clad canyon and venture on to the base of 40-foot Paradise Falls, with bonus waterfalls and a shady oak picnic stop on your return.

Start: At the west end of the Mesa Trail parking area by the information kiosk and map
Elevation gain: 400 feet
Distance: 2.8-mile loop
Difficulty: Moderate to strenuous (while some portions are easy, others are steep, rugged with uneven steps and lots of them or no steps at all)
Hiking time: About 1 hour 45 minutes
Age range: 5 years+
Seasons/schedule: Year-round, but best when water is flowing, ideally winter and spring (impacted by seasonal rainfall). However, heavy rains can lead to washouts and temporary closures of some of these trails. Call or check online for updates.
Fees: Free
Trail contact: Conejo Open Space Conservation Association, Ranger

Headquarters, Conejo Recreation and Parks District, 403 W. Hillcrest Dr., Thousand Oaks 91360, (805) 381-2741, www.conejo-openspace.org
Trail surface: Dirt, clay, gravel
Land status: Regional park
Nearest town: Thousand Oaks
Dogs: Dogs on leash
Toilets: At far side of Meadows Picnic Area and at nearby Wildflower Playfield you will pass on your drive in along Avenida de Los Arboles
Other trail users: Mountain bikers and equestrians on portions of these trails
Maps: Map of Wildwood Regional Park Trails at www.conejo-openspace .org.
Special considerations: Steep drop-offs without railings, uneven surfaces with tripping hazards

FINDING THE TRAILHEAD
From US 101 at Thousand Oaks, take exit 45 following signs for Lynn Road. Drive 2.5 miles north on Lynn Road, then turn left (west) onto Avenida de Los Arboles. Follow Avenida de Los Arboles 1 mile to its end where you'll see the parking and staging area for the Mesa Trail. The signed trailhead is at the west side of the parking area. **GPS:** N34 13.14' / W118 54.12'

THE HIKE

Though the hike begins on what feels like a less-than-interesting, wide service road populated by many locals there to walk their dogs or get in their mountain biking miles, it will soon take a turn for the more interesting at 0.2 mile. Ignore the first trail offshoot to your left and at the trail marker instructing you to continue straight for Lizard Rock and Paradise Falls; you'll instead turn left to proceed southwest.

Soon after, a wooden fence railing will appear to your right, and you'll follow along to where, at 0.5 mile, it opens onto a narrower dirt trail with the sign for "Moonridge Trail." Soon, you'll begin descending into a canyon with perennial wildflowers and prickly pear cacti—be sure to watch for the special prickly pear pads or "paddles," which sometimes form in the shape of hearts.

Steep steps and switchbacks bring you down to a dry/seasonal creek before ascending back up the other side. At only 0.8 mile, you'll arrive back at the top of this canyon,

A view of Paradise Falls and North Fork Conejo Arroyo from above.

where a wide dirt road forms a T with your trail: the North Tepee Trail. Proceed to your left (south) toward the large, vintage Tepee structure with (possibly shaded) benches and a drinking fountain.

At the teepee (0.9 mile), you'll follow the clearly marked trail sign toward your right (northwest) for Paradise Falls. In only 0.2 mile you'll leave the dirt road and turn left (south) onto the narrow, dirt Wildwood Canyon Trail, which begins a quick descent with

Stairs and switchbacks make for a quick descent on the Moonridge Trail.

switchbacks to the North Fork Arroyo Conejo and the Paradise Falls lower viewing area. Follow the trail down the steps through the picnic tables toward the water to get the best view from below on this side of the creek (it will be partially obstructed by rock from this view, but it is still lovely and the sounds are wonderful).

When ready, retrace your steps up through the lower viewing and picnic areas, then continue to your right (southeast) up toward the upper viewing area, where you'll get a different view of the falls from above and see additional small waterfalls upstream.

Top: Hiking along the refreshing Wildwood Canyon Trail in spring with a contrast of desert-hearty cacti and flowing water.
Bottom: The Rivoli family resting at lower Paradise Falls.

Continue southeast along the North Fork Arrojo Conejo and a sycamore- and oak-shaded section of Wildwood Canyon Trail, with three sheltered picnic tables awaiting at 1.6 miles. At 1.7 miles, you'll come to a three-way split in the trail; continue straight along the Wildwood Canyon Trail toward the Meadows Picnic Area.

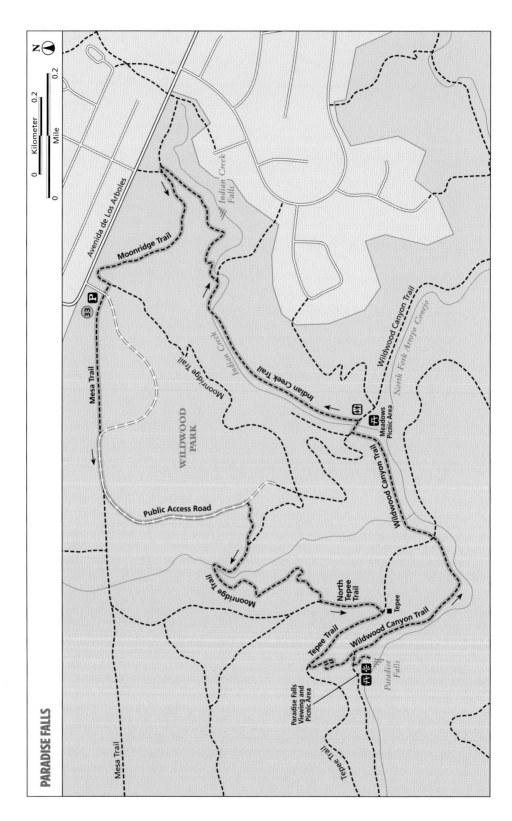

PARADISE FALLS

N

Kilometer
0   0.2   0.2

0   0.2
Mile

Avenida de Los Arboles

33 P

Moonridge Trail

Indian Creek Falls

Mesa Trail

Moonridge Trail

Indian Creek

Indian Creek Trail

WILDWOOD
PARK

Public Access Road

Moonridge Trail

Mesa Trail

Wildwood Canyon Trail

North Fork Arroyo Conejo

Meadows
Picnic Area

Wildwood Canyon Trail

North Tepee
Trail

Tepee Trail

Tepee

Wildwood Canyon Trail

Paradise Falls
Viewing and
Picnic Area

Paradise Falls

Tepee Trail

At 1.9 miles go right to cross the bridge (Meadows Picnic Area and restrooms are on the other side), then take the immediate left at the sign for Indian Creek Trail and Arboles Avenue. From here, you'll follow along the south side of Indian Creek until wooden steps lead you down to the water to cross on wooden planks at 2.2 miles. You'll continue along the north side of Indian Creek, working your way up a respectable slope (at some points a 15 percent grade) and several wooden steps set into the hillside.

But at 2.3 miles, be sure to take a breather and step over toward the edge of the trail (with caution!) to view the beautiful Indian Creek Waterfall below. When ready, continue toward the end of Indian Creek Trail (you'll see Avenida de Los Arboles ahead) and make a hairpin left (southwest) onto a section of Moonridge Trail that will lead you through oak trees and back to the opposite end of the parking area where you began.

MILES AND DIRECTIONS

0.0   Start at the Mesa Trail trailhead.

0.2   Skip the first left, then take the second left (southwest), ignoring the sign that says "straight to Lizard Rock and Paradise Falls."

0.5   Turn right (west) onto Moonridge Trail.

0.8   Take a left (south) onto North Tepee Trail (service road).

0.9   Go right (northwest) at the Tepee.

1.1   Turn left (south) at the Paradise Falls sign onto Wildwood Canyon Trail.

1.2   Arrive at the lower falls; when ready, retrace your steps up and continue southeast on Wildwood Canyon Trail.

1.3   Arrive at the upper waterfall viewpoint.

1.6   Take a break at the picnic area.

1.7   Proceed straight on the center trail at the three-way split.

1.9   Take a hard right (southeast) to cross the bridge, then left (north) at the sign for Indian Creek Trail.

2.2   Veer left (north) to stay on Indian Creek Trail.

2.3   Reach the Indian Creek Waterfall overlook.

2.5   Indian Creek Trail ends; take a hard left (southwest) to follow Moonridge Trail.

2.8   Arrive at the opposite end of the parking area where you started and continue to your car.

Note: There are many variations you can make on this hike and opportunities to extend it (e.g., continue past the falls toward Lizard Rock and Eagle Point for a longer loop), but this 2.8-mile version is a great introduction to the location, combining a nice variety of scenery with a healthy elevation gain and ideal spots to stop and take snack breaks.

34 CHARMLEE WILDERNESS LOOP

After closure due to the devastating Woolsey Fire of 2018, this beloved Malibu wilderness park has reopened to the public and is springing back to life with abundant wildflowers, resilient live oaks, and thriving wildlife.

Start: At the information kiosks (conveniently behind the restrooms)
Elevation gain: 443 feet
Distance: 3-mile loop
Difficulty: Moderate/strenuous (some rocky, steep sections)
Hiking time: About 1.5 hours
Ages on foot: 4 years+
Seasons/schedule: Year-round, but trails are mostly exposed so avoid in very hot weather. Park is closed on red flag warning days (fire risk); call trail contact for info.
Fees: Day-use fee has been lifted but may return
Trail contact: City of Malibu, 23825 Stuart Ranch Rd., Malibu 90265-4861, (310) 317-1364, www.malibucity .org

Trail surface: Dirt, rock, sand
Land status: Wilderness
Nearest town: Malibu
Dogs: Yes, on leash
Toilets: At trailhead
Maps: Map at information kiosk at trailhead
Other trail users: Some sections of this hike allow mountain bikers and equestrians
Special considerations: Rattlesnakes and coyotes are present in this area. Loose rocks and tree roots call for mindful footwork in some sections.
Gear suggestions: Bring layered clothing to meet the extremes—what can start as a cold, misty morning here can turn to full sun and heat before hike's end.

FINDING THE TRAILHEAD

From US 101 (Ventura Freeway), take exit 36 for Kanan Road, following it south for 6.1 miles. Turn right (west) briefly onto Mulholland Highway, but stay left to continue onto Encinal Canyon Road for another 3.5 miles. Turn left again to stay on Encinal Canyon Road a final 1.5 miles, before turning right onto Carmichael Road for the short drive to the staging area at this road's end. Or from the Malibu area and CA 1 (Pacific Coast Highway), turn north on Encinal Canyon Road. In 3.8 miles turn left onto Carmichael Road and follow for 0.3 mile to the staging area.
GPS: N34 3.42' / W118 52.74'

(**Note:** Your navigation system may try to route you via CA 23 if it believes it will save you 2 minutes of drive time, but it won't feel like it—especially not if you have anyone prone to carsickness riding with you.)

THE HIKE

From the information kiosk, start your journey heading uphill (northwest), following the old, wide service road past the (presently closed) small nature center. At 0.3 mile make a hard left (south) where, if it isn't too hazy, a magnificent view over the hills to the Pacific will open up to you—and soon you'll enjoy wide-open views from both sides of the trail. This can be a lucky place for spotting wildlife, especially in the early morning and before the trails get busy (keep the binoculars handy!).

At 0.5 mile you'll take the right (southwest) fork beneath the water tower and enjoy a gradual downhill stretch toward the ocean before a few ups and downs. At 0.7 mile you'll arrive at a T; take the right (west) to continue downhill watching for the very faint (and

View down the coast to Point Dume.

easy to miss!) singletrack snaking off through the grass on your left just 0.1 mile farther (the Matt Kouba Trail).

You'll descend into a canyon, which can be thick with wildflowers in spring and offers the dappled shade of coastal live oak year-round. Look for lupine, hummingbird sage, monkeyflower, and giant coreopsis, to name just a few.

As you begin climbing from the canyon, continue straight on the main path until you find yourself at a T (1 mile), then head right (southwest) onto West Meadow Trail for a

Top: Coyote sighting near the water tower during a morning hike.
Bottom: Finishing the Black Forest Trail with lofty views over the Pacific.

relatively flat stretch through open space until you see a notable tree-topped knoll rising ahead of you (sometimes called the Black Forest). Watch for the narrow (and likely unmarked) Black Forest Trail at 1.2 miles, which splits off to the right side (west) of the knoll. Follow it past a series of large, pitted boulders and oak trees, where you might like to stop and enjoy a shaded snack and water break (and perhaps some small-scale bouldering).

CAPTURED BY THE CRITTER CAM!

Check out the "Animals of Charmlee Wilderness Park" channel on YouTube, where you can see trailcam footage of some of the most fascinating creatures who also hike the hills of this beautiful area. Some of the footage captured includes bobcats, gray foxes, striped skunks, mule deer, and quail.

A quail poses atop a rock, cleverly matching the Santa Monica Mountains in the background.

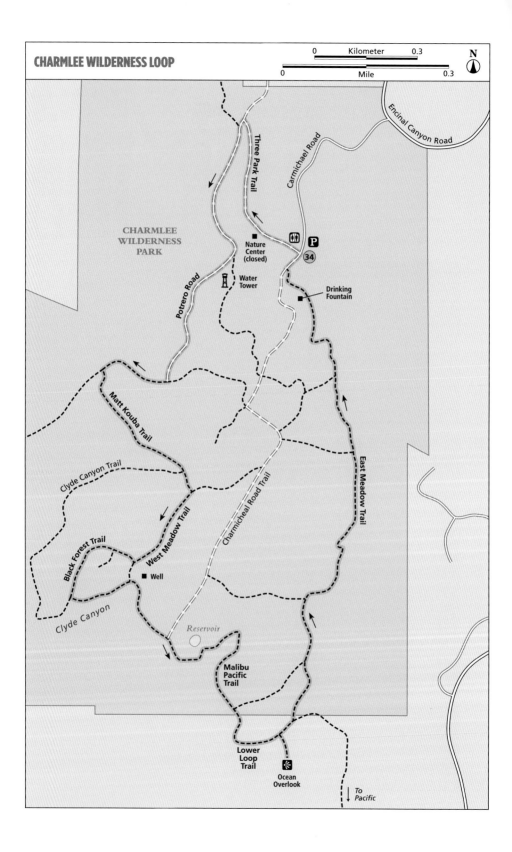

CHARMLEE WILDERNESS LOOP

0   Kilometer   0.3

0   Mile   0.3

N

Encinal Canyon Road

Three Park Trail

Carmichael Road

CHARMLEE
WILDERNESS
PARK

Nature
Center
(closed)

P
34

Water
Tower

Drinking
Fountain

Potrero Road

Matt Kouba Trail

Clyde Canyon Trail

East Meadow Trail

West Meadow Trail

Charmicheal Road Trail

Black Forest Trail

Well

Clyde Canyon

Reservoir

Malibu
Pacific
Trail

Lower
Loop
Trail

Ocean
Overlook

To
Pacific

Trek on as the gentle descent provides a sudden spectacular view up the coast as you continue around this delightful side loop trail. Stay to the left (east) at the fork to rejoin the West Meadow Trail again at 1.5 miles near a landmark rusty, old well spigot left over from cattle-ranching days.

As you continue southeast, you'll eventually come upon a far more dramatic relic from the ranch: a deep, circular, cement-lined (and empty) reservoir. Follow the trail as it curves around the top of the reservoir with dramatic views over the ocean and, this time, *down* the coast (have a seat on the memorial bench if it's available). When it's clear, you'll see the golden crescent of Zuma Beach curving in the distance.

At 1.8 miles you'll stay to the right (south) and continue toward the short spur that's the official "ocean overlook" (in case there weren't enough chances to overlook the ocean already on this hike). When ready, rejoin the trail and continue right (northeast/north), following the East Meadow Trail inland, avoiding any left (west) turns along the way.

After 2.5 miles you'll encounter a steep, rocky section that may call for an extra reward snack for the youngest hikers conquering this climb. At 2.9 miles you'll pass a drinking fountain and water spigot (good for thirsty dogs) to your left (west) just before joining the service road and finishing at the information kiosk where you started.

MILES AND DIRECTIONS

0.0	Start northwest at the kiosk, up the hill.
0.3	Take a hard left (south).
0.5	As you approach the water tower, stay right at the fork (southwest).
0.7	Turn right (west) at the T.
0.8	Go left (south) onto Matt Kouba Trail.
1.1	Turn right (southwest) onto West Meadow Trail.
1.2	Veer right (west) at the knoll side loop (Black Forest Trail / Clyde Canyon Trail).
1.5	Rejoin West Meadow Trail near the well and continue southeast.
1.7	Reach the old reservoir.
1.8	Go straight (south) to stay on the Lower Loop toward the overlook.
2.0	Arrive at the official ocean overlook; continue north on the Lower Loop.
2.3	Continue north (straight) as the trail becomes East Meadow and follow all the way back toward the trailhead.
3.0	Return to the kiosk at the trailhead.

Note: Some trails you see on older maps may no longer exist, while others may still not be fully opened—or marked—at the time of your visit. Keep the mile-by-mile directional cues handy, and remember, the Pacific Ocean is *not* to your west along this coastline, but rather to your south.

35 WENDY-SATWIWA LOOP

Stretch your legs among the serene rolling hills of the Santa Monica Mountains with views of Boney Mountain, seasonal creek crossings, and a visit to a Native American cultural center and Chumash demonstration village.

Start: At the trailhead on Potrero Road
Elevation gain: 249 feet
Distance: 2-mile lollipop
Difficulty: Moderate (mostly easy, but a steep section with up to 22 percent grade and possible bridgeless creek crossings)
Hiking time: About 45 minutes
Ages on foot: 3 years+
Seasons/schedule: Trails open year-round; Satwiwa Native American Indian Culture Center open 9 a.m. to 5 p.m. weekends only
Fees: Free
Trail contact: Santa Monica Mountains National Recreation Area, 26876 Mulholland Hwy., Calabasas

91302, (805) 370-2301, www.nps.gov/samo
Trail surface: Dirt and rock
Land status: Natural area managed by the National Park Service
Nearest town: Thousand Oaks
Dogs: Dogs allowed on these trails on a 6-foot leash but not on some connecting trails
Toilets: Restrooms at Satwiwa Culture Center
Maps: Online at www.nps.gov/samo/
Other trail users: Connecting trails may be used by mountain bikers and equestrians
Special considerations: Rattlesnakes, mountain lions

FINDING THE TRAILHEAD

From Thousand Oaks, take US 101 north for 3.2 miles to exit 45 for Lynn Road. Turn left (south) onto Lynn Road and continue 4 miles to South Wendy Drive. Turn left (south) onto Wendy Drive and drive 0.6 mile until it forms a T at Potrero Road. Look for a space among the plentiful nose-in parking along the south side of Potrero Road. Look for the open section of barbed-wire fence near where Wendy Drive meets Potrero (across the street from a church) and, just beyond, you'll see informational trail signs greeting you. **GPS:** N34 9.24' / W118 57'

THE HIKE

The Wendy Trail starts out fairly level leading you from the edge of Potrero Road into a refuge of open greenspace with Boney Mountain in the distance. At 0.1 mile an equestrian bypass trail crosses your path, as you continue straight (south), then slightly down toward a grouping of oak trees and across a small, seasonal creek. When it's flowing, you may need to do a little rock-hopping here.

At 0.3 mile take the left (south) fork onto the Windmill Trail, where the trail begins to climb steeply—up to a 22 percent grade makes for a fast and furious elevation gain. In another 0.1 mile, you'll stay left again to continue on the Windmill Trail as it finally levels out and you can enjoy views of nothing but rolling hills, trails, and the Santa Monica Mountains ahead of you—and the knowledge that you've already climbed to the highest and most challenging point of this hike.

At 0.5 mile you'll turn right (west) onto the Satwiwa Loop Trail and follow it 0.6 mile all the way to the Satwiwa Native American Indian Culture Center. This area, along

Late winter wildflowers and lush green grass fill the Satwiwa Natural Area.

with Boney Mountain and the wilderness area to the south, is considered sacred by the Chumash and is open to hikers only, making wildlife viewing all the more likely along the way (watch for golden eagles, foxes, bobcats, and coyotes, among others). In wet seasons, you may have one or two more small creek crossings in this section.

You'll also see a traditional Chumash home structure called an 'ap on the south side of the trail, part of the outdoor Chumash demonstration village, just before arriving at the Culture Center building. These round structures are built from willow poles bent into a dome-shaped frame, then covered with bent and woven tule reeds. Large 'aps could be divided into rooms inside by hanging woven mats.

The Chumash people lived in this area as many as 13,000 years ago—several thousand years before the first Europeans arrived. Satwiwa, a Chumashan word meaning "the

Top: A traditional Chumash dwelling on display along the Satwiwa Loop Trail.
Bottom: A coyote stalks its dinner at dusk in the Satwiwa Natural Area.

bluffs," was the name of a Chumash village near today's Culture Center by the same name; Sycamore Canyon, which passes from south of Satwiwa Natural Area through Point Mugu State Park toward the Pacific, was an important trade route for the Chumash people.

Today, the Satwiwa Native American Indian Culture Center helps increase awareness of and appreciation for the area's first people. It also helps keep Native American culture, art, and traditions alive through family-friendly demonstrations, art shows, presentations, and workshops held year-round.

A view of Boney Mountain from the Satwiwa Native American Indian Culture Center.

After visiting the 'ap and exploring the Satwiwa area, retrace your steps down the Satwiwa Loop Trail to the first trail leading off to your left (northeast) and up a hill. A marker simply labels this section "Recreation Trail" as it connects to the Wendy Trail in another 0.1 mile. Stay to your right to continue northwest all the way back to the first section of the Wendy Trail you started on, then retrace your steps to the parking area on Potrero Road.

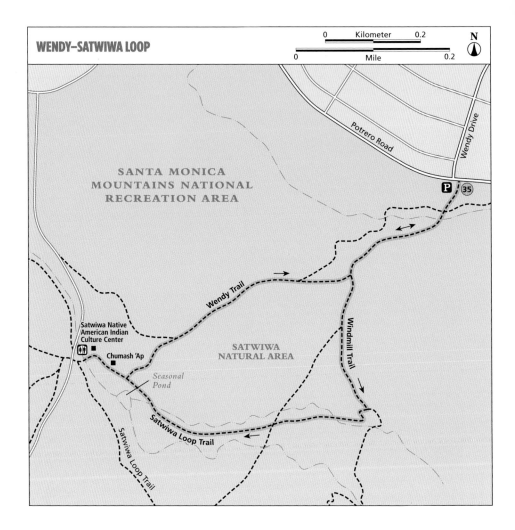

MILES AND DIRECTIONS

0.0   Start at the trailhead.

0.1   Continue straight across the bypass trail.

0.3   At the fork turn left (south) onto Windmill Trail.

0.4   Veer left (southwest) to stay on Windmill Trail.

0.5   Turn right (west) onto Satwiwa Loop Trail; continue straight for 0.6 mile to the Culture Center.

1.1   Retrace Satwiwa Loop Trail for 0.1 mile.

1.2   Turn left (northwest) onto "Recreational Trail."

1.3   Continue straight (northwest) onto Wendy Trail, until rejoining first section.

2.0   Return to the trailhead.

36 FERN DELL NATURE TRAIL TO GRIFFITH OBSERVATORY

Hike from a hidden LA oasis up to the historic landmark observatory, enjoying lofty views over the city from one of America's largest urban parks. And surprise! You'll discover photo ops with the Hollywood Sign along the way. An alternative, mostly shaded, 0.8-mile route here is ideal for toddlers and younger children.

Start: At the Ferndell Park gated entrance, at the corner of Fern Dell Drive and Black Oak Drive
Elevation gain: 613 feet
Distance: 2.5-mile lollipop, or an alternative easy 0.8-mile out-and-back
Difficulty: Moderate/difficult
Hiking time: About 1 hour 25 minutes
Ages on foot: 8 years+ for the full 2.5-mile hike, 2 years+ for the abbreviated 0.8-mile round-trip hike
Seasons/schedule: Year-round, but be mindful of heat as the trails above Fern Dell are quite steep and exposed.
Fees: Free
Trail contact: Friends of Griffith Park, PO Box 27573, Los Angeles 90027-0573, info@friendsofgriffithpark.org, https://friendsofgriffithpark.org

Trail surface: Paved and then packed dirt
Land status: City of Los Angeles
Nearest town: Los Angeles
Dogs: Dogs on leash
Toilets: At playground and at the top near the observatory parking lot
Maps: Griffith Park map online at www.laparks.org/griffithpark/pdf/GriffithParkMap.pdf
Special considerations: The steep descent with packed dirt and minimal scree can be surprisingly slippery, so caution enthusiastic kids who may be excited to race back down the hill.
Gear suggestions: Lightweight picnic blanket for relaxing and snacking with views on the Observatory lawn

FINDING THE TRAILHEAD

From I-5, take exit 141 and merge onto Los Feliz Boulevard, continuing southwest for 2.3 miles. Turn right (north) onto Fern Dell Drive. In less than 500 feet, you'll see the gated entrance to Ferndell Park at the corner of Fern Dell Drive and Black Oak Drive. Look for free street parking here along Fern Dell Drive.

From US 101 Southbound, take exit 8C for Gower Street and turn left (north) onto Gower Street, crossing over US 101. Then turn right (east) onto Franklin Avenue and continue for 0.8 mile to N. Western Avenue, where you'll turn left (north), followed quickly by a slight right (northeast) onto Los Feliz Boulevard and immediate left (north) onto Fern Dell Drive. **GPS:** N34 6.57' / W118 18.46'

THE HIKE

This hike begins in a lush oasis tucked between a Los Angeles neighborhood and the edge of Griffith Park's open space. Once fed exclusively by natural springs, the sycamore-shaded stream and surrounding canyon was an important site for the Gabrielino–Tongva people (recognized as the aboriginal tribe of the Los Angeles Basin) for thousands of years.

Hiking up the West Observatory Trail toward Griffith Observatory.

As you stroll along the shady, paved, first 0.3 mile of the Fern Dell Nature Trail, you'll find yourself surrounded by lush ferns and tropical foliage—some native as well as other varieties added for atmosphere beginning in 1914 when health tourists began frequenting the location to sip what they believed were healing waters from the stream.

Along the way you'll pass a series of small bridges crisscrossing the stream, small grottos and burbling mini waterfalls, and other features created through the 1920s and finally

Top: The hike begins with Fern Dell Nature Trail, a stroller-friendly, shady oasis.
Bottom: The Rivoli kids pause to take in the view of the Hollywood Sign from the West Observatory Trail.

completed by the Civilian Conservation Corps during the Great Depression. Though it became sluggish over time, the stream is kept flowing today thanks to a recycled water project—though sipping its nonpotable waters is highly discouraged!

At 0.3 mile you'll exit the gate at the opposite end of the landscaped area and proceed straight on the dirt path until you see a playground, picnicking area, and finally restrooms

Looking back at the Greek Revival Dome of Griffith Observatory from the East Observatory Trail.

on your left. This is your last call for restrooms, drinking fountains, benches, and shade before hitting the open trail. (Option: If you choose the shorter version of this hike, the bridge behind the restrooms is your outbound destination and where you'll turn back when ready.)

Just beyond the restrooms, you'll see the trail continue straight as the East Observatory Trail with a glimpse of Griffith Observatory above. This will be your return route. Bear left instead (northwest), crossing over a pedestrian bridge and making an immediate right onto the well-marked West Observatory Trail. Here begins the climb—some 520 feet in elevation gain over your remaining 0.7 mile to the top.

Enjoy views of iconic Griffith Observatory above the hillside chapparal and oaks as you climb. When the brush eventually opens up on your left (northwest), be sure to pause for a water break—and behold the world-famous Hollywood Sign, which has suddenly come into view. You may want to get a photo of your entourage with the sign in the distance.

At 1 mile the East Observatory Trail connects with the West, and clear days will bring a fantastic view from this juncture with downtown LA in the distance (another great photo op for your family). Bear left (east here, but eventually south and then north) onto the Griffith Observatory Trail and continue up the steep, final 0.2 mile, ignoring any lesser offshoot trails, until the trail ends at the east end of the observatory building.

Whether or not your outing includes a visit inside Griffith Observatory (admission is free, check griffithobservatory.org for hours), you can enjoy great views from the lawn out front and from the outdoor observation deck accessed from the west side of the building. The lawn is also a popular picnicking spot and a great place to rest and celebrate your climb with some snacks.

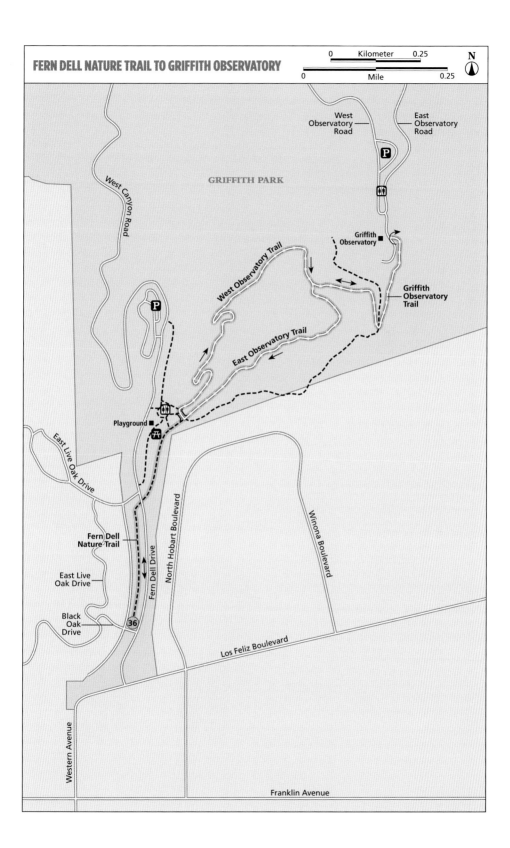

FERN DELL NATURE TRAIL TO GRIFFITH OBSERVATORY

0 Kilometer 0.25

0 Mile 0.25

N

West Observatory Road

East Observatory Road

GRIFFITH PARK

West Canyon Road

West Observatory Trail

Griffith Observatory

Griffith Observatory Trail

East Observatory Trail

Playground

East Live Oak Drive

North Hobart Boulevard

Winona Boulevard

Fern Dell Nature Trail

East Live Oak Drive

Black Oak Drive

36

Fern Dell Drive

Los Feliz Boulevard

Western Avenue

Franklin Avenue

When you're ready to return, follow the Griffith Observatory Trail back down to the junction of East and West Observatory Trails, taking care with the steep sections where it's easy to slip on the hard-packed trail. At the junction make a hard left (southeast) onto the East Observatory Trail and continue downward enjoying entirely new views until you reach Ferndell Park once again and return to the Fern Dell Nature Trailhead where your adventure began.

MILES AND DIRECTIONS

0.0 Start at the trailhead.

0.3 Exit the landscaped section through the gate; continue straight.

0.4 Turn left (northwest) to cross over the pedestrian bridge and follow the sign to proceed right (northeast) up the West Observatory Trail.

1.0 West and East Observatory Trails join together; continue left (east) and uphill on the Griffith Observatory Trail.

1.4 Arrive at Griffith Observatory; backtrack to West and East Observatory Trail junction when ready.

1.8 Turn left (southeast) onto the East Observatory Trail; continue to and through Fern Dell.

2.5 Arrive back at Fern Dell Trailhead.

BIRDS OF A FEATHER

Today's 4,200-acre Griffith Park was merely a ranch outside the city limits until its first ostriches arrived. In 1885 Rancho Los Feliz landowner Charles Griffith and naturalist Charles Sketchley decided to capitalize on the latest fashion trend that could fetch $5 a feather from the gangly birds—the equivalent of $136 today. Soon after, the entrepreneurial Griffith, Sketchley, and other local landowners created the Ostrich Farm Railway to transport Angelenos and tourists from downtown LA to the hilly open space of the ranch for a chance to see the strangely exotic birds from Africa and enjoy the open space and trails of the ranch. The ostrich farm lasted fewer than 5 years, but eventually its railway morphed into the first linking Los Angeles to Santa Monica, and a stretch of it became the winding section of Sunset Boulevard near Echo Park.

37 **INSPIRATION POINT**

Hike from the historic estate of film star and humorist Will Rogers up this popular gateway to the Santa Monica Mountains, to where a 360-degree view over Los Angeles and the Pacific Ocean await. Then catch a peaceful, partly shaded "secret trail" back for variety.

Start: At the sloped trail starting up at the east edge of the parking area near the tennis courts
Elevation gain: 328 feet
Distance: 2-mile loop
Difficulty: Moderate
Hiking time: About 50 minutes
Ages on foot: 4 years+
Seasons/schedule: Year-round
Fees: Day-use fee $$ or California Explorer Pass
Trail contact: California State Parks, PO Box 942896, Sacramento 94296, (310) 230-2017, www.parks.ca.gov/willrogers

Trail surface: Dirt, rock, gravel
Land status: State historic park
Nearest town: Pacific Palisades
Dogs: Yes, on a 6-foot leash
Toilets: Near trailhead
Maps: Printable map included in brochure at www.parks.ca.gov/willrogers
Other trail users: Mountain bikers allowed on main path/service road
Special considerations: Tripping hazards from rocks and roots, also possible poison oak, rattlesnakes

FINDING THE TRAILHEAD

From Santa Monica, take CA 1 North / Palisades Beach Road north for 1 mile, then turn right (west) onto Chautauqua Boulevard. In 1 mile take a slight right onto Sunset Boulevard and continue for 0.5 mile. Turn left onto Will Rogers State Park Road and proceed to the first parking area past the entrance booth. The trail starts at the east end of this parking area. **GPS:** N34 3.24' / W118 30.6'

THE HIKE

Start up the unmarked trail and take an immediate right (east) to follow the level, eucalyptus-lined trail behind the Will Rogers ranch house and museum. After a glimpse of the polo field, you'll arrive at the white fence and steps up to the horse stables—enjoyed by the Rogers family from 1926 to 1935 and still in use today by equestrians and riding enthusiasts. As you reach the top of the steps, turn left (west) to follow the trail past the "Inspiration Loop Trail" sign and kiosk with map of the "Backbone Trail" area.

The wide, dirt trail begins to climb immediately, and as you follow around the first curve, you'll find you're already gaining views above tree-filled neighborhoods, across to downtown LA. At 0.5 mile, as you round the southern bend, your view then stretches on to the Pacific.

As the easy-to-follow, wide path continues northward toward the top, you'll enjoy views of the Santa Monica Mountains as well as the adjacent undeveloped expanse of Topanga State Park. At 0.8 mile you may notice an unmarked, minor trail intercepting from the right—the trail you'll be on as you make your way back down the hill. For now, continue straight on the wide main path.

At 1 mile a wooden sign for "Inspiration Point" greets you near the top, keeping you on the right track—to the right (east), straight up the hill—as additional hiking trails

Enjoy peaceful views over LA as you hike up the Inspiration Loop trail.

connect just below. In this final 0.1 mile of your ascent, you'll arrive at what's clearly the top of the hill, with 360-degree views of the city, hills, and ocean. Rest your legs at one of the benches or picnic tables as you reward yourselves with a well-deserved snack.

(**Note:** Older maps show a southward continuation from the top, but that section of trail is no longer in service.) Instead, you'll backtrack from the top to the final "Inspiration Point" sign on the main trail and, this time, continue to your right (north), slightly downhill, until you see the wooden information kiosk at the junction with the Backbone Trail and a continuation of the Inspiration Loop.

Now, look southeast, in the opposite direction of the kiosk, across the wide, main trails to find the narrow, barely noticeable beginnings of a humble trail. Just a short distance down this trail, you'll see a sign for "no bicycles." Continue down the quiet path, occasionally overhung with shady trees and flowering white ceanothus, and you're on your way down the Betty Rogers Trail.

Top: View from the top at Inspiration Point.
Bottom: Looking out toward the Santa Monica Mountains and Topanga State Park.

At 1.7 miles you'll pass through fence posts and rejoin the main trail once again, continuing left (south) downhill for just 0.1 mile, until you see a narrow dirt trail slip off to your left (southeast) beside a leaning fence. This trail gives you different views over the Will Rogers estate as you complete your final journey downhill.

At 2 miles you'll cross the original, wide path, and simply stay straight to return to the parking area, now visible just below you.

MILES AND DIRECTIONS

0.0   Start at the east edge of the parking area.

0.8   Continue straight, uphill on the main trail.

1.0   Stay right (east) at the "Inspiration Point" sign.

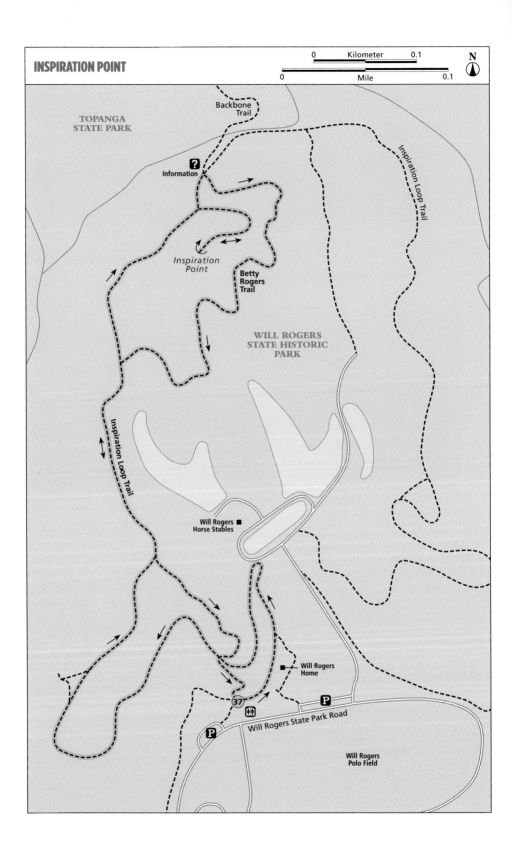

INSPIRATION POINT

0   Kilometer   0.1

0   Mile   0.1

N

TOPANGA
STATE PARK

Backbone
Trail

Inspiration Loop Trail

? Information

Inspiration
Point

Betty
Rogers
Trail

WILL ROGERS
STATE HISTORIC
PARK

Inspiration Loop Trail

Will Rogers ■
Horse Stables

Will Rogers ■
Home

37

P

P

P

Will Rogers State Park Road

Will Rogers
Polo Field

The beginning of the less-traveled and lovely Betty Rogers Trail.

1.1	Arrive at the summit; backtrack to the "Inspiration Point" sign.
1.2	Take a hard right (east) onto the unmarked Betty Rogers Trail.
1.7	Rejoin the main trail for 0.1 mile downhill (south).
1.8	Turn left (southeast) using the narrow, unmarked trail.
2.0	Crossing your original path, stay straight to return to parking area.

38 EATON CANYON WATERFALL

This shortcut version of the longer hike from the Eaton Canyon Nature Center makes a rapid descent to the most interesting and shady portion of the trail, which leads you through a narrow canyon with many bridgeless creek crossings to a lovely 40-foot waterfall and tranquil pool. **Note:** This route is recommended for weekdays due to weekend parking restrictions. On weekends you'll need to park and hike from the Eaton Canyon Nature Center.

Start: At the gated Mount Wilson Toll Road (service road) on the east side of Pinecrest Drive
Elevation gain: 354 feet
Distance: 2-miles out-and-back (3.5 miles if hiked from the Nature Center)
Difficulty: Moderate because creek crossings may require boulder-hopping and scrambling and a steep return from the canyon
Hiking time: About 1 hour
Ages on foot: 4 years+
Seasons/schedule: Weekdays year-round, but be mindful of heat. Street parking is prohibited on weekends.
Fees: Free
Trail contact: Angeles National Forest, 701 N. Santa Anita Ave.,
Arcadia 91006, (626) 574-1613, www .fs.usda.gov/angeles/
Trail surface: Paved, dirt, sand, and rock
Land status: National forest
Nearest town: Altadena
Dogs: Yes, on leash
Toilets: None
Maps: USGS 7.5-minute Mount Wilson
Other trail users: Mountain bikers share first section of trail (service road)
Special considerations: Slippery rocks when creek is flowing; shoes likely to get wet during creek crossings, so bring a backup pair for after your hike.

FINDING THE TRAILHEAD

From Pasadena, head east on I-210 for roughly 2.5 miles and take exit 28 for Altadena Drive. Turn left (north) onto Altadena Drive and continue for 2.7 miles. Turn right (northwest) at Crescent Drive and take the next right (northeast) onto Pinecrest Drive and begin looking for street parking spaces, which can be used weekdays only. Then look on the east side of Pinecrest Drive for the imposing, tall, metal fencing across a service road, with signs warning about rock slides and helping to keep the canyon clean. Where the door-sized metal gate within this is propped open for hikers and bikes, enter and begin. **GPS:** N34 11.46'/W118 6.3'

THE HIKE

Start with a steep descent down the paved Mount Wilson Toll Road (a gated service road), which soon turns to dirt as you pass the signed fork for the Altadena Crest Trail on your left (north) at a tenth of a mile. Continue on the service road, crossing over the bridge, with Eaton Canyon and Creek below.

At 0.2 mile you'll take the right fork at the "Eaton Canyon Trail" sign, and at 0.3 mile be sure to take the hard right to hike north (upcanyon to the waterfall) on Eaton Canyon Trail and not south to the Nature Center. You'll soon pass beneath the bridge you crossed on your way down as the canyon narrows, then at 0.4 mile you'll pass an old cement spillway, which crosses the creek.

Eaton Canyon Waterfall on a hot summer day.

Enjoying the shade of Eaton Canyon en route to the waterfall.

Continue north between large boulders, enjoying the shade of a variety of deciduous trees as the trail meanders near the creek. Depending on the timing of your visit, Eaton Creek may be full and rushing or dry in this area. As you continue upcanyon from here, you may need to rock-hop and get creative with creek crossings (and wet shoes) as necessary, while on drier visits you can simply walk up the dry creek bed. Either way, you'll continue following the informal path of the creek toward its source.

At 0.9 mile the canyon bends to the left (west), and it may be easiest to finish your approach to the falls on the left (south) side of the creek. Hopefully, your ears will already hum from the sounds of water dropping 40 feet into a shallow pool, but even in lower-flow stages, Eaton Canyon Waterfall presents a beautiful contrast of trickling water against mossy rocks in this typically arid climate.

Find a good boulder by the base of the waterfall and enjoy the scenery before retracing your steps to the trailhead.

Watch for hummingbirds as you pass an old tree tobacco while hiking down Mount Wilson Toll Road.

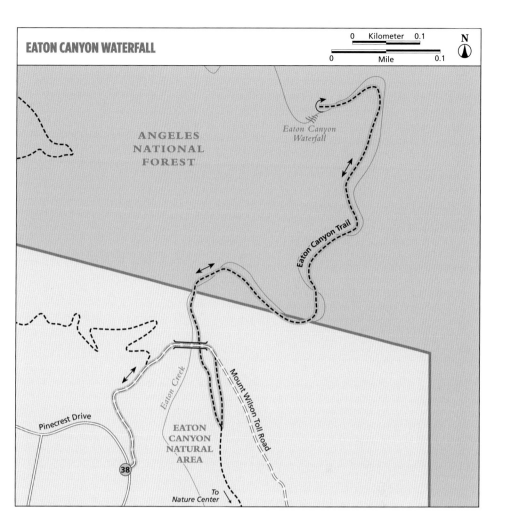

ANGELES
NATIONAL
FOREST

*Eaton Canyon
Waterfall*

Eaton Canyon Trail

Eaton Creek

Mount Wilson Toll Road

Pinecrest Drive

38

EATON
CANYON
NATURAL
AREA

To
Nature Center

MILES AND DIRECTIONS

0.0   Start at the trailhead.

0.2   Take the right fork down (southwest) at the sign.

0.3   Take a hard right (north) toward the bridge.

0.4   Continue past the spillway, following the creek upcanyon.

1.0   Arrive at the waterfall; backtrack when ready.

2.0   Return to the trailhead.

Hike through this shady San Bernardino Mountains woodland as you make your gradual way up to a picturesque clearing with a glimpse of Lake Arrowhead and some fun boulders to climb and rest upon. Come prepared: This is the perfect spot for a picnic.

Start: Signed trailhead at south end of parking area
Elevation gain: 394 feet
Distance: 1.9-mile out-and-back, with options to extend or create a loop
Difficulty: Easy to moderate
Hiking time: About 50 minutes
Ages on foot: 3 years+
Seasons/schedule: Early spring through fall. Trail closes for snow in winter months, so check local weather conditions if uncertain.
Fees: Free (though donations to the trust for their continued efforts are appreciated, https://sbmlt.net/)

Trail contact: The San Bernardino Mountains Land Trust, PO Box 490, Lake Arrowhead 92352, (909) 867-3536
Trail surface: Dirt and rock
Land status: Land trust
Nearest town: Blue Jay
Dogs: Yes, on leash
Toilets: None
Maps: No official map (take a photo of this one with you)
Other trail users: Joggers

FINDING THE TRAILHEAD

From Crestline, take Lake Gregory Drive southeast for 2.2 miles to CA 189. Turn left (east) onto CA 189 and continue 2.7 miles to Grass Valley Road. Turn left to drive north on Grass Valley Road for 0.7 mile watching for the first paved turnoff to your right (east). Turn onto the small, paved entrance and proceed into the parking area for both the Will Abell Memorial Trail and Arrowhead Ridge Picnic Area. The signed trailhead is at the south end of the parking area. **GPS:** N34 14.9' / W117 13.14'

THE HIKE

As you find your way to the signed trailhead at the south end of the parking area, take note of the wide swath of pavement leading straight up the hillside here, gated off to vehicles and blocked with boulders. Obviously, this is not the beautiful forest scenery you brought your family to enjoy. Yet this abandoned road, now sprouting weeds in its cracks as nature strives to reclaim it, is an important reminder of how close this 80-acre parcel of land came to being fully paved and developed for luxury vacation homes—and closed to the public entirely.

Starting up the dirt trail, to the right of the abandoned road, you'll immediately enjoy the shade of a variety of trees. With its thriving mix of black oaks, incense cedars, white firs, ponderosas, and sugar pines, this is considered by scientists to be the best remaining example of the original forest setting of the Lake Arrowhead region.

After passing the first couple small switchbacks, stay to your right (west/southwest) to follow a large switchback, continuing up the hill and staying on the main trail. Watch for the thick undergrowth of cedar saplings rising vigorously from what you might never guess is a section of the failed subdivision.

Peek through the trees of a quiet clearing for a view of Lake Arrowhead.

Looking around now, as you continue your gradual climb along the peaceful forest trail and take in the fragrances of cedar and fir trees, it may be hard to believe this area was abandoned by developers and left littered and strewn with construction debris. But thanks to generous donors and hundreds of hours of work by volunteers (including the trail's namesake), the area has been restored and returned to the public to enjoy for generations to come.

However, it's not just the humans who can be thankful for this gift of open space. This protected parcel also supports three beloved and at-risk species of forest dwelling creatures: the San Bernardino flying squirrel, California spotted owl, and southern rubber boa.

A TINY-BUT-MIGHTY FLIER

The San Bernardino flying squirrel has extra skin that stretches from its wrists to ankles, like a built-in parachute. Though it must venture down to the forest floor each night in search of truffles, it can glide more than 300 feet between trees in a single flight, traveling great distances through the forest without ever touching the ground.

Top: Incense cedar saplings spring to life after major restoration efforts.
Bottom left: Great seating options (and easy bouldering) await at the top of the hill.
Bottom right: This thriving, mixed coniferous forest is considered the best example of its kind remaining in the San Bernardino Mountains.

The final 0.3 mile to the top of this trail is the steepest (13 percent to 18 percent grade), but at 0.9 mile it suddenly levels off at a T. Follow the trail to your right (south) until you find yourself in a small, almost circular forest clearing rimmed by tall trees. Cross the clearing, watching to your left (east) for glimpses of Lake Arrowhead through the pines and black oak trees.

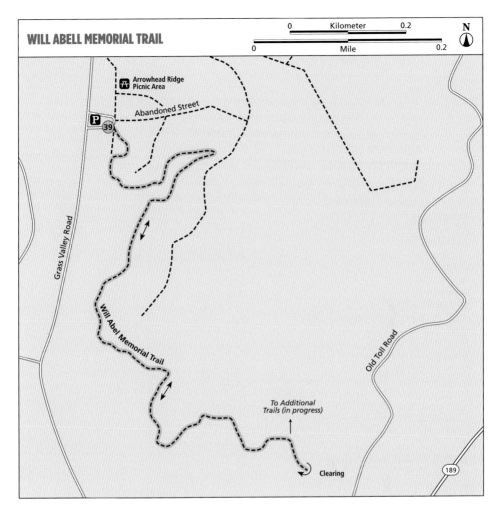

There is plenty of level ground in this clearing for you to pitch a picnic blanket or find the perfect perch on any of the boulders at the edge. Enjoy your snacks and picnic lunch before retracing your steps down the trail to the trailhead.

Option: For variety you can continue your hike north from the T, exploring additional trails (in progress) that will take you through both forest scenery and some lingering remnants of the almost-subdivision, though be warned these trails and connections are not always clearly marked.

MILES AND DIRECTIONS

0.0 Start at the trailhead.

0.3 Stay right (west) for a long switchback.

0.9 Arrive at a T at the top of the trail; go right (south) to a clearing; retrace your steps when ready.

1.9 Return to the trailhead.

40 BIG BEAR LAKE WOODLAND TRAIL

With the help of your free interpretive map from the Big Bear Discovery Center, you'll enjoy an easy-to-moderate hike through Jeffrey pine, black and canyon oak, and ironwood, all while learning about sixteen numbered sites along this well-marked loop. Bonus boulders provide fun climbing opportunities for the bigger kids, while benches make it easy to stop and rest little legs if needed.

Start: Signed trailhead at east edge of parking area
Elevation gain: 236 feet
Distance: 1.5-mile loop
Difficulty: Easy to moderate
Hiking time: About 50 minutes
Ages on foot: 3 years+
Seasons/schedule: June through Sept depending on when the snow melts and returns
Fees: Adventure Pass or America the Beautiful pass required to park in lot, but street parking is free along both sides of Highway 38 at the entrance here
Trail contact: Big Bear Discovery Center, 40971 North Shore Dr.,
Highway 38, Fawnskin 92333, (909) 382-2790
Trail surface: Dirt and rock
Land status: National forest
Nearest town: Fawnskin
Dogs: Yes, on leash
Toilets: At parking lot and the Big Bear Discovery Center
Maps: Pick up your free interpretive map of this trail at the Big Bear Discovery Center 5 minutes away (1 mile east on North Shore Drive)
Other trail users: Mountain bikers
Special considerations: Snakes—maybe even rattlesnakes—possibly in the rocky areas

FINDING THE TRAILHEAD

From Big Bear City, drive east on CA 38 / North Shore Drive. Continue 0.2 mile past the Stanfield Cutoff and turn right (north) onto Woodland Road at the sign for the Lake Woodland Trail. If you don't have an Adventure Pass or America the Beautiful pass (required for the parking lot), take advantage of the free parking along North Shore Drive here. The trailhead is on the east side of the official Woodland Trail parking lot. **GPS:** N34 15.79' / W115 59.94'

THE HIKE

Before starting this hike, stop off at the Big Bear Discovery Center, just 1 mile east on North Shore Drive, where you can pick up the Woodland Trail interpretive guide (in case all are out at the trailhead) and the Big Bear Valley Hiking Trails guide with additional trail descriptions and an overview map of trails in the area—both are free and the restrooms are much nicer here than the vault toilets at the trailhead.

You can do this hike either clockwise or counterclockwise, but for the easiest time following the printed guide along with the numbered trail signs, you'll start at the signed trailhead on the east side of the parking area. From the first exhibit—an ancient Western juniper estimated to be 1,500 years old—you'll find yourselves reimagining this area from a totally different perspective from that of today's Big Bear tourists. Imagine living

The Rivoli kids find the ideal location for a picnic along the Woodland Trail.

Top: Rotting log to you . . . all-you-can eat buffet to a lizard!
Bottom: Mountain mahogany (aka ironwood) produces these feather-like curly seeds that help plant themselves through their corkscrew design.

here when this tree was young, when the native Yuhaviatam people may have woven loose, stringy bark from this very tree into blankets, shoes, and clothing.

As you move along, the exhibits will invite you to also consider the plants and natural features of the trail from the perspective of the local wildlife—and even some of the plants themselves. A downed tree may look like little more than a rotting log at first

Holy tree trunk! This Jeffrey pine helps feed an entire colony of acorn woodpeckers each winter.

Would you guess this mound of sticks is a multi-roomed mansion built by a woodrat?

glance, but on closer inspection you may see the squiggly lines left by larval grubs that live beneath the bark. Look again and you may spot a lizard that lives off the larvae and other bugs that call the log home.

Another favorite along this trail is called "The Kitchen Pantry," a well-used Jeffrey pine tree that supports an entire colony of acorn woodpeckers each winter. In early summer the hundreds of holes in the trunk may look empty. But by fall, these nut-sized "cupboards" will be packed full of acorns again, ready to feed the woodpeckers both acorn meat and the bonus insects and grubs that may be eating their acorns.

Continue around in the counterclockwise loop, learning to identify the common trees and native plants of this dry woodland, discovering a packrat's nest, and looking for tracks from the wild animals that hike through here themselves at night en route to the lake for a drink of water. And as the interpretive guide reminds visitors, those marvelous granite boulders along the trail can be fun to climb on—but they are also the habitat of lizards and *snakes*. So do use caution when climbing, and keep your furry friend on-leash.

The hike ends on the opposite side of the parking area at just over 1.5 miles.

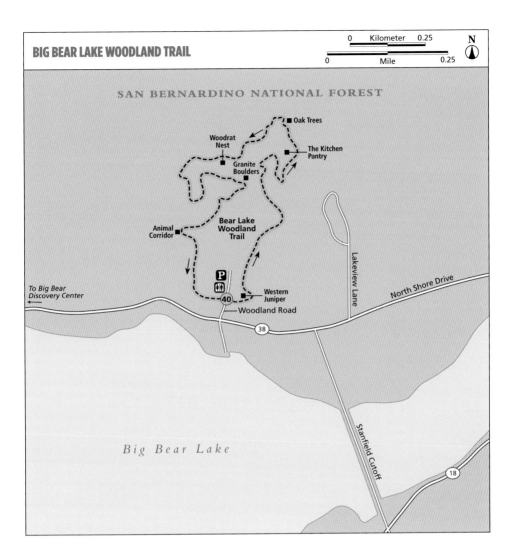

BIG BEAR LAKE WOODLAND TRAIL

MILES AND DIRECTIONS

0.0 Start at the trailhead at the east side of the parking area.

1.5 The loop trail ends at the west side of the parking area.

Point Loma at low tide with
Mexico's Los Coronados Islands
in the distance.

SAN DIEGO AND SURROUNDING AREA

While San Diego is the most compact of the regions covered in this guide, it's home to a startling 27,109 acres of open space within its city limits alone—including 210 miles of multiuse trails. Both in the city and throughout greater San Diego County, hikers enjoy a wide variety of outdoor landscapes to explore, owed in part to the fascinating geologic history of the San Diego area.

In just the past 20,000 years, San Diego has seen dramatic sea level changes—imagine heading to the beach during the previous ice age when sea level was 400 feet lower than it is today! Over the past million years or so, the Rose Canyon fault, which passes right through San Diego Bay and the heart of today's downtown San Diego, has also shaped (and reshaped) this landscape, altering the courses of rivers and streams and uplifting layers of ancient seabeds that formed tens of millions of years ago.

The resulting seaside cliffs, peaceful estuaries, rugged mountains, and riparian corridors make San Diego a hiker's paradise, with great options for year-round excursions. These five hikes, ranging from easy to strenuous, will lead your family on some of San Diego's best and most memorable trails for kids, from sea level (or below if you time it right) to the highest summit in San Diego.

41 ANNIE'S CANYON

A leisurely stroll along a wildflower-filled and protected lagoon takes a turn for adventure with a slot-canyon side loop your family won't soon forget—and may immediately want to repeat! Note that Annie's Canyon is extremely popular with local families, so for the best experience and the least-crowded canyon, plan your visit for a nonholiday weekday.

Start: The wide trailhead with steps down at the end of North Rios Avenue
Elevation gain: 180 feet
Distance: 1.7-mile lollipop
Difficulty: Strenuous in the canyon with some necessary scrambling, moderate on the switchback alternate route to the top (and route down from canyon), and easy on all other segments
Hiking time: About 50 minutes
Ages on foot: 3 years+ with some assistance
Seasons/schedule: Year-round, though the canyon closes during heavy rain and is not advisable in very hot weather
Fees: Free
Trail contact: Nature Collective, PO Box 230634, Encinitas 92023, (760) 436-3944, https://thenaturecollective.org

Trail surface: Packed and loose sand
Land status: Ecological reserve
Nearest town: Solana Beach
Dogs: Dogs allowed on leash on all trails except Annie's Canyon Trail itself. If hiking with a dog, you can have one family member take Fido up the switchback alternate trail to greet you at the top of the canyon trail.
Toilets: None
Maps: No official map; use this map (take a phone photo for your visit)
Special considerations: Tree roots could be tripping hazards for excitable kids in some areas.
Gear suggestions: Bulky daypacks are not advisable in the canyon due to extremely narrow passages (barely the width of a pair of shoes). Sunglasses can be helpful to protect eyes from sand blowing or getting brushed from the canyon walls.

FINDING THE TRAILHEAD

Using a navigation system to take you to Annie's Canyon or Annie's Canyon Trail may direct you to a different trailhead, such as the Holmwood Canyon Trailhead, where neighborhood parking is even tighter and nonresidents are not allowed to drive on Holmwood Lane, adding at least 0.2 mile of walking down a gravel street before reaching that trailhead. Here's the better way:

From I-5 North or South, take exit 37 for Lomas Santa Fe Drive in the direction of Solana Beach (west / toward the ocean). Continue on Lomas Santa Fe Drive 0.8 mile, then turn right (north) onto North Rios Avenue for approximately 0.8 mile. Find free neighborhood street parking anywhere near the end of the street. The trailhead is marked with wide steps down at the center of the end of North Rios Drive. **GPS:** N33' 0.22' / W117 16.2'

THE HIKE

The hike begins at the end of North Rios Avenue with a few wide cement steps down, followed by a brief stroll through the patchy shade of riparian scrub. In 0.1 mile the trail turns to packed sand, coursing through coastal sage scrub and seasonally flowering shrubs that are popular with hummingbirds.

Pausing to look back down the canyon trail during a rapid ascent.

Just beyond lies the freshwater-brackish marsh that brims the San Elijo Lagoon. This 979-acre ecological reserve is one of San Diego's largest wetlands and a birder's paradise. But for kids, it's what's waiting at 0.6 mile that they're most likely to remember—and ask to revisit.

Once families pass through the gate to Annie's Canyon (closed during heavy rain), they are met with a choice. As the sign indicates, they can choose the trail to the left, a switchback route up to the viewpoint (moderate with dogs allowed on leash). Or they

Top: View from the switchback trail looking over San Elijo Lagoon at low tide with the Pacific in the distance.
Bottom: For the grand finale of your slot canyon tour, climb these narrow ladders to reach the top.

can head to the right to traverse the slot canyon up to the viewpoint (difficult and no dogs allowed).

Adventurous souls, stay to the right where the canyon rises steeply and suddenly to your sides with its walls of Torrey Sandstone formed roughly 46 million years ago. At 0.7 mile the claustrophobic have one last chance to reconsider the henceforward one-way route as they arrive at the "No dogs allowed" sign beside a narrow, steep, sandy slit—the continuation of the canyon trail.

ANNIE'S CANYON

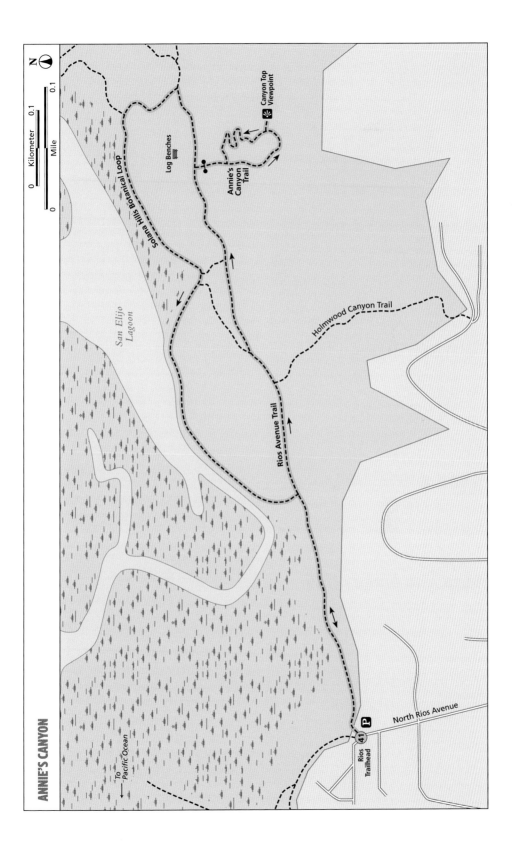

N

0   Kilometer   0.1

0   Mile   0.1

San Elijo Lagoon

Solana Hills Botanical Loop

Log Benches

Annie's Canyon Trail

Canyon Top Viewpoint

Holmwood Canyon Trail

Rios Avenue Trail

To Pacific Ocean

P

41

Rios Trailhead

North Rios Avenue

Some passages will be no wider than a pair of adult-size shoes, and little ones will likely need a boost at some steep, sandy transitions, such as the offshoot trail about to appear to your left. This quick detour takes you into a small, natural cave where you can get a quick feel for the graffiti that marred the entire canyon before cleanup and restoration efforts kicked off with a generous donation from Annie herself, the woman for whom the canyon is now named (this patch was left as a reminder).

Once you return to the main trail, you'll continue ascending through the slot canyon until finally the steel spines of narrow, near-vertical ladders appear before you. Climb on up to finish your canyon adventure with a great view over San Elijo Lagoon toward the Pacific.

When ready, proceed down the switchback trail back to the kiosk where you earlier turned in to the canyon. Just beyond the kiosk, natural benches (tree trunks) await in the shade of a eucalyptus grove here in case you're ready for a snack break or brought a picnic along.

From here, you'll continue your counterclockwise route, turning left (north) at the Gemma Parks Loop sign, and following the Solana Botanical Loop trail nearest the water. At 1.5 miles you'll rejoin the Rios Avenue Trail, and then retrace your steps to the trailhead at North Rios Avenue.

The canyon trail narrows and the climbing begins.

MILES AND DIRECTIONS

0.0 Start at wide steps down to the trail.

0.2 Stay right/straight at the fork (east).

0.3 Holmwood Canyon Trail joins from the right (south); continue straight.

0.6 Reach the information kiosk, turn right (south) to pass through the gate and follow the sign, staying right (south) for the canyon route.

0.7 "No Dogs" sign; go left (northeast) into narrow canyon.

0.9 Arrive back at kiosk, go right (east), then a quick left (north) at "Gemma Parks Loop" sign.

1.0 Ignore offshoot trails; continue west along the main trail nearest the water.

1.5 Rejoin Rios Avenue Trail and follow back out to where you started.

1.7 Arrive back at the trailhead.

42 GUY FLEMING TRAIL

Set high above the Pacific in the midst of a 2,000-acre State Natural Reserve, this easy (and popular!) trail takes you past the rare Torrey pine and abundant native wildflower species, with short spurs to panoramic viewpoints up and down the Pacific Coast.

Start: At the signed trailhead at the edge of Torrey Pines Park Road, just above the roadside parking spaces
Elevation gain: 52 feet
Distance: 0.8-mile lollipop
Difficulty: Easy
Hiking time: About 30 minutes
Ages on foot: 2 years+
Seasons/schedule: Year-round, but expect a line for park entry between 11 a.m. and 3 p.m. in peak summer months. (Park opens at 7 a.m. and closes just before sunset.)
Fees: $$$ day-use fee or California Explorer Pass

Trail contact: Torrey Pines State Reserve, 12600 North Torrey Pines Rd., San Diego 92037, (858) 755-2063, https://torreypine.org
Trail surface: Packed and loosening packed sand
Land status: State natural reserve
Nearest town: La Jolla and Del Mar
Dogs: No dogs
Toilets: At park entrance and uphill from this hike at the visitor center
Maps: Park trail map available at https://torreypine.org
Special considerations: Steep cliffs—make sure kids respect the trail boundaries.

FINDING THE TRAILHEAD

From US 101, turn west into the Torrey Pines Beach Parking South Lot. From the toll booth, continue driving 0.5 mile along Torrey Pines Park Road to the turnout for nose-in car parking (limited spaces). You will see the signed Guy Fleming trailhead at the edge of the road, just above these spaces. **GPS:** N32 55.38' / W117 15.3'

Note: This can be an extremely busy park and trail on weekends and peak vacation seasons. Parking spaces near the trailhead are limited, and parking elsewhere will mean walking along the side of the road to get back to the trailhead—not desirable with kids in particular. If at all possible, plan your visit to avoid the crowds. And if you can't park at the trailhead, consider pulling over to drop off most of your party at the trailhead—they can wait for you on the benches just 0.1 mile down the trail.

THE HIKE

Torrey pines are a local celebrity—known to grow only in the San Diego area and on two of the Channel Islands. Today, they are classified as a rare and endangered species and can be found in only three locations: 1) the vicinity of the Torrey Pines State Natural Reserve area, 2) in a small area in nearby Del Mar, and 3) on Santa Rosa Island in Channel Islands National Park (considered a different subspecies from its mainland cousins).

As you start this hike, you'll find a Torrey pine greeting you right at the signed trailhead. These elegant pines can be recognized by their long needles clustered in groups of five, and they can grow to about 25 feet in their native habitat.

Walk west on the trail and you'll quickly come to the first of some informational signs and benches you'll find along the route. Among these, you'll see a sign explaining how the trail's namesake Guy Fleming ". . . is to Torrey Pines what John Muir was to

A view up the coast from the north overlook on the Guy Fleming Trail.

the High Sierras." In 1916 he began working to help people understand the significance of the species and to help protect these pines and this important area from uncontrolled recreation and visitors who used Torrey pines as firewood.

Between the fascinating ripples in the sandstone formations you'll pass as you start the hike and the breathtaking views up and down the coast at the north and south overlooks, it's easy to see why city dwellers were eager to camp, picnic, and carouse atop the iconic cliffs. Fortunately, in 1921 Guy Fleming became the first resident caretaker of "Torrey

Top: Prickly pear cacti with a view over the Pacific.
Bottom left: Get a close-up look at some of the fascinating sandstone formations found at
Torrey Pines from this easy trail.
Bottom right: Strolling south above the Pacific on the Guy Fleming Trail.

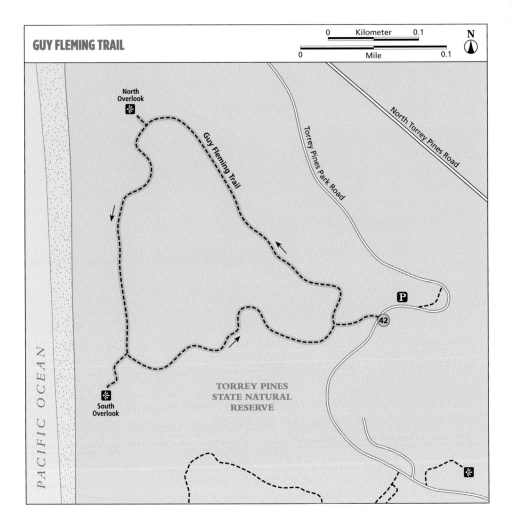

North Overlook

Guy Fleming Trail

Torrey Pines Park Road

North Torrey Pines Road

P

42

PACIFIC OCEAN

South Overlook

**TORREY PINES
STATE NATURAL
RESERVE**

Pines Reserve," establishing its first network of trails for visitors to enjoy—and ensuring they did so responsibly.

As you come around the south bend of the loop at 0.75 mile, you'll retrace the earlier section of trail as you return to the trailhead. Enjoy exploring the park and beach while you're here, and if interested in exploring another trail, head up to the visitor center to ask for a recommended trail for your group that day, as conditions (and suitability) can vary on other trails here.

MILES AND DIRECTIONS

0.0 Start at the trailhead; at the fork take the right trail heading north or clockwise around the loop.

0.3 Reach the north overlook.

0.5 Arrive at the south overlook.

0.8 Return to the trailhead.

43 LOS PEÑASQUITOS CREEK WATERFALL

This easy, partially shaded hike follows a creek through a riparian corridor with two bridge crossings and a small waterfall, all set in an easily accessed urban oasis of protected habitat for frogs, herons, egrets, mallards, mule deer, and more.

Start: At the signed trailhead on Camino Del Sur
Elevation gain: 95 feet
Distance: 4.6-mile lollipop
Difficulty: Easy, other than scrambling on rocks (and possibly crossing) at the waterfall
Hiking time: About 1 hour 45 minutes
Ages on foot: 3 years+
Seasons/schedule: Year-round, best in early spring for optimal water flow and supreme frog song
Fees: Free
Trail contact: Friends of Los Peñasquitos Canyon Preserve, PO Box 26523, San Diego 92126, www .penasquitos.org; park ranger for trail info (858) 538-8066

Trail surface: Dirt and mud, with gravel at entrance
Land status: City- and county-owned preserve
Nearest town: San Diego
Dogs: Dogs welcome on 8-foot leash
Toilets: Across street from trailhead at Peñasquitos Creek Park
Maps: Printable maps at www .penasquitos.org/trails-maps
Other trail users: Equestrians share this route; mountain bikers share the North Main Trail
Special considerations: Poison oak, snakes, rushing water during high flow at the waterfall
Gear suggestions: Good shoes for getting muddy (or wet if you hope to cross at the waterfall)

FINDING THE TRAILHEAD

From I-5 (north or south), use exit 33 for Carmel Valley Road and follow signs at exit to merge onto CA 56 East. Continue east for 6.4 miles, then take exit 7 and turn right (south) onto Black Mountain Road. In 0.4 mile turn right (west) onto Park Village Road, and continue 1.6 miles to Camino Del Sur. Turn left (south) onto Camino Del Sur and watch for the free street parking spaces along the right side of the street. You'll see the information kiosk and trailhead near the first of these parking spaces. **GPS:** N32 56.34' / W117 9.12'

THE HIKE

Before setting out down the trail, check the information kiosk at the trailhead for any important announcements about the area, including possible trail closures (you can also call ahead to the park ranger). During the wet winter season, many trails in the area flood, helping the life cycles of the flora and fauna that this preserve was established to protect—and the reason it isn't filled with houses like the neighborhood you'll see just beside this entrance (a good talking point for young hikers).

Tromping through the seasonal swimming holes of the Pacific tree frog or trampling over the off-trail vegetation to get around the puddles could defeat the very purpose of this preserve, so be sure to respect any closures and take alternate routes where needed.

Top left: Watching for wildlife on Carson's Crossing.
Top right: A section of the small waterfall(s) area on Peñasquitos Creek.
Bottom: Listening to a fantastically loud chorus of Pacific tree frogs.

From the trailhead, you'll walk downhill on a dirt service road leading southwest past patches of prickly pear cacti. At 0.1 mile stay right at the fork (west). You'll return on the other fork when you close the loop. At 0.2 mile you'll turn left (south) onto a narrower trail marked for equestrians and hikers—but not bicycles.

Follow this short connector trail toward the brushy wall of trees forming the riparian corridor along Peñasquitos Creek, and turn right to continue west, following the north side of the creek. Here and there you'll see established turnouts to get closer to the water's edge, where you might spot mallards, wading egrets, or a great heron.

LOS PEÑASQUITOS CREEK WATERFALL

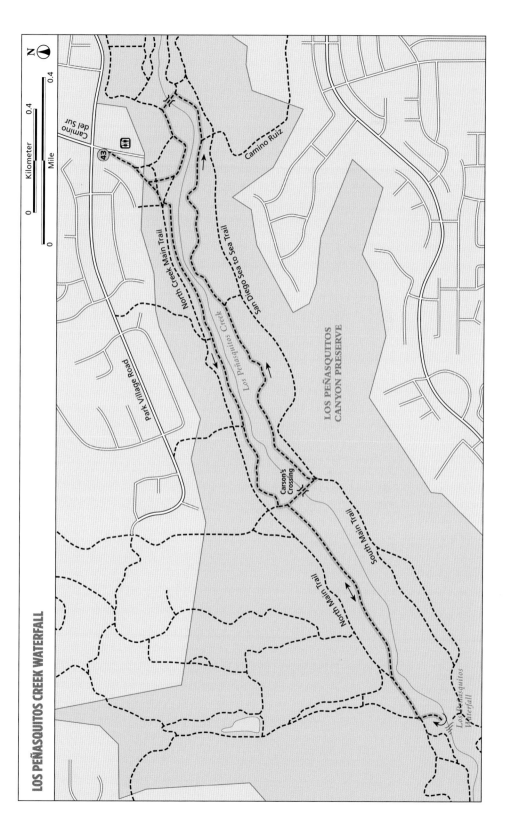

Around 0.5 mile the oaks and brush form a tunnel-like canopy around you. Pause and wait a quiet moment to see if you can hear any frogs or songbirds. Then continue beside the quiet creek, passing in and out of shade. At 1.2 miles you'll see a trail split off to the left (southeast), which leads to Carson's Crossing—one of the boardwalk bridges you'll later take over Peñasquitos Creek. For now, you'll continue straight (southwest), listening for the sounds of rushing water.

At 1.8 miles the North Main Trail merges and you'll soon see bike racks and an information kiosk for the waterfall and trails. Follow along the wooden fence toward the creek, where rocky steps lead toward large boulders along the water. Pick a spot for your family to perch itself, overlooking the creek as it flows and splashes over and between the descending rocks in a modest waterfall.

The water flow varies by season and by year, so what you find on one visit may be quite different from the next. On lower-flow visits and with older children, you may be comfortable crossing the creek toward the steep stone steps leading up on the other side. If so, you can cross and use the South Main Trail from here to start your journey back (see map).

Assuming the falls are flowing nicely, enjoy them from this side, then simply retrace your steps back to Carson's Crossing to cross over the creek. As the boardwalk ends, stay left (northeast) to follow the trail closest to the south side of the creek (marked "no bicycles").

Around 3 miles, stop. Be silent. If you're lucky, amid this strangely jungle-like setting of squatty palms, you may suddenly hear the goose-bumpy vibrato of a chorus of Pacific tree frogs.

Continue eastward along the south side of the creek. At 4 miles, the Camino Ruiz Trail splits off to the south, but you'll continue straight (east) for 0.2 mile more to where there is a sudden option to make a sharp left turn (northwest)—which won't feel intuitive. But you'll know you're on the right track when another wooden bridge quickly appears, leading you back across Peñasquitos Creek.

After crossing, you'll intercept a sign pointing right for the North Main Trail, but you'll instead go left (west), soon rejoining the original trail where you started and finishing at the trailhead.

MILES AND DIRECTIONS

0.0	Start at the trailhead.
0.1	Turn right (west) at the fork.
0.2	Turn left (south) onto the connector trail, then right (west) onto the creekside trail.
1.2	Pass the turnoff for Carson's Crossing; continue straight.
1.9	Turn left (south) at the kiosk and sign for the waterfall.
2.0	Arrive at the waterfall; when you're ready, backtrack to Carson's Crossing.
2.8	Turn right (southeast) to use Carson's Crossing then take an immediate left (east) onto the creekside trail.
4.0	Pass the Camino Ruiz turnoff; stay straight (east).
4.2	Take a hard left (north) and cross the bridge, then take another left (west).
4.4	Rejoin the first section of trail.
4.6	Return to the trailhead.

44 COWLES MOUNTAIN TRAIL

This popular hike to the highest point in the city of San Diego presents a great workout over a short distance (especially for little legs!) that's rewarded with ever-improving views until gaining the summit. On clear days, this 360-degree view includes the Laguna and San Ysidro Mountains, Lake Murray, Los Coronados Islands of Mexico, Point Loma, and downtown San Diego.

Start: At the Cowles Mountain staging area sign and stonework steps behind restrooms
Elevation gain: 905 feet
Distance: 3-mile out-and-back
Difficulty: Strenuous
Hiking time: 1.5 to 2 hours
Ages on foot: 5 years+ (some really big steps up or scrambling for those with little legs on top of the big elevation gain)
Seasons/schedule: Year-round, but plan around hot weather as there is no shade. Because of the trail's popularity, it's most enjoyable Mon through Thurs on nonholidays.
Fees: Free
Trail contact: Mission Trails Regional Park Visitor and Interpretive Center, One Father Junipero Serra Trail, San Diego 92119, (619) 668-3281, https://mtrp.org/
Trail surface: Rocks, rock face, gritty sand/gravel
Land status: Regional park
Nearest town: San Carlos
Dogs: Yes, on leash
Toilets: At trailhead
Maps: Printable Mission Trails trail map PDF available at https://mtrp.org/
Special considerations: Large uneven rocks and steep surfaces, heat in hot weather, possibility of rattlesnakes
Gear suggestions: Trekking poles for those who like them, sturdy-sole footwear for constantly uneven surfaces

FINDING THE TRAILHEAD

From eastbound I-8, use exit 10 for College Avenue. Turn left (north) onto College Avenue and continue for 1.3 miles. Turn right onto Navajo Road (northeast) and continue 2 miles to Golfcrest Drive, where a left turn (north) is followed by an immediate right turn into the parking area for the Cowles Mountain Staging Area. If the parking lot is full, look for free parking along the street. **GPS:** N32 48' / W117 1.8'

THE HIKE

The hike begins at the prominent staging area and stonework steps behind the restrooms. With 905 feet of elevation to gain in the next 1.5 miles, be sure to start at a reasonable pace for everyone in your group.

The well-marked trail alternates between some fairly smooth sections, occasional steps, and more technical rocky terrain. Trail markers let you know your progress up the mountain at 0.25-mile intervals—each a great cause for high fives and rehydration before making your way to the next.

By the first of these, the 0.25-mile trail marker, you'll already see a glimmer of the Pacific and have lovely views toward San Miguel Mountain and over Lake Murray. Just past the 0.5-mile marker, you'll find some large boulders on the view-side of the trail,

Top: The view toward San Miguel Mountain at 0.25 mile.
Bottom: Large boulders on the view-side of the trail make great resting spots.

which make a great place to rest and have a snack break either on the way up or down if the top is very busy.

At 0.8 mile you'll pass a sign to your right (east) for the Barker Way Trail, which leads downhill from this point. On your uphill journey to the summit, it's easy to see this is not your route, but be sure everyone in your group will be watching for it on the downhill journey, to make sure they stay on the right track (literally to the right, i.e. south).

Just past the 1.25-mile trail marker, the trail splits and you'll stay left (southwest) to continue your final stretch up and around to the top of Cowles Mountain, elevation 1,591 feet. Take in the 360-degree view of San Diego County and beyond and use the informational display to help identify the landmarks around you.

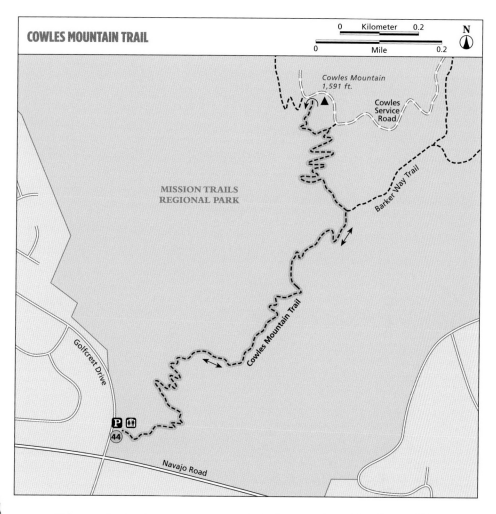

0   Kilometer   0.2

0   Mile   0.2

N

Cowles Mountain
1,591 ft.

Cowles
Service
Road

Barker Way Trail

MISSION TRAILS
REGIONAL PARK

Cowles Mountain Trail

Golfcrest Drive

P   44

Navajo Road

When ready, simply retrace your steps back down to the trailhead—you'll be amazed how much faster the return trip goes!

MILES AND DIRECTIONS

0.0   Start at the trailhead.

0.8   Continue straight, passing Barker Way Trail.

1.3   Stay left (west) at the trail split.

1.5   Arrive at Cowles Mountain summit; backtrack when ready.

3.0   Return to the trailhead.

Cowles Mountain Peak at 1,591 feet above sea level.

Accessible only during very low tides (0.7 feet or less), this hike takes you along exposed shelves, pools, and coves teeming with fascinating marine critters in one of the best protected, rocky, intertidal areas in all of California.

Start: At the signed trailhead leading southwest from the Cove Trail parking area
Elevation gain: 112 feet
Distance: 1-mile lollipop
Difficulty: Moderate to strenuous (the Coastal Trail itself has many steep steps along the way, but going down to the lower tidepools also requires agility and some scrambling). Small children may need assistance climbing back up some sections of rock.
Hiking time: 1 to 2 hours depending on how much tidepool exploration or picnicking you do
Ages on foot: 4 years+ with some assistance likely needed to get up and down from the rocky shelves at lowest tides
Seasons/schedule: Best in fall and winter months when the lowest tides occur during daytime hours (details in The Hike). The tidepool trail closes at 4:30 p.m. year-round.
Fees: $$$ day-use fee, National Parks Pass, or Every Kid Outdoors Pass for fourth graders. For groups of 10 or more visiting during 0.7 feet tides or lower, a tidepool permit is required.

Trail contact: Cabrillo National Monument, 1800 Cabrillo Memorial Dr., San Diego 92106-3601, (619) 557-5450, www.nps.gov/cabr
Trail surface: Dirt, sand, wooden stairs, and rock
Land status: National monument and state marine reserve
Nearest town: San Diego
Dogs: Yes, on a 6-foot leash on Coastal Trail only; dogs are not allowed in the tidepool area.
Toilets: At lower tidepool parking area
Maps: A map with the Coastal Trail and overview of Cabrillo National Monument is online at www.NPS.gov/cabr/. The lower Tidepool Trail is informal and may change slightly with each visit. Shown here is a suggestion of how your own route may look at low tide.
Special considerations: Cliffs, coastal surges, slippery rocks. Cell phone service is not available at the tidepools.
Gear suggestions: Rafting sandals with great traction as the rocks can be slippery (and your feet are likely to end up wet).

FINDING THE TRAILHEAD

From southbound I-5, take exit 20 for I-8 toward El Centro / South Rosecrans Street. Stay to the right for 0.7 mile, following signs for Rosecrans Street, then merge (briefly) onto Camino Del Rio West. Continue straight onto Rosecrans Street for another 2.6 miles to Cañon Street. In 1.3 miles use the left lanes to turn onto Catalina Boulevard. In 1 mile Catalina Boulevard becomes Cabrillo Memorial Drive, and you'll continue 2.2 miles to and through the paid entrance gate to Cabrillo National Monument. Just past the entrance, turn right onto Cabrillo Road and follow it 1 mile down past the Tidepool Parking area (stop here for restrooms if needed) and continuing north up to the Sea Cove Parking area. The signed trailhead is at the southwest end of the parking area. **GPS:** N32 40.2' / W 117 14.4'

THE HIKE

The Point Loma Tidepool Trail is accessible only during very low tides (0.7 feet or lower), which typically fall during daytime hours only in winter and fall. And the *best* time for this hike is during the negative tides that occur in the winter months. For optimal upcoming tides and times to plan your hike, visit the "Rocky Intertidal Zone" learning section at www.nps.gov/cabr/, where you'll also find fun photos and a time-lapse video showing how dramatically this area changes with the tides.

Start your hike at the signed trailhead southwest of the Cove Parking area, taking note of any current advisories posted there and important rules for visitors to this protected area. Two rules that children should especially be aware of include: 1) no collecting (don't bring any buckets or nets) and 2) leave animals where you find them—animals at the tidepools *can* be touched, but they should be touched gently with only one finger.

As you head south along this first stretch high above the Pacific, look for sleepy harbor seals who enjoy the undisturbed rocks below during low tide. Assuming your hike starts closest to the lowest tide time of your visit, you'll take the fork toward the ocean (right/southwest) at 0.1 mile, leaving the Coastal Trail that continues straight for your later return.

Though your chosen trail may appear to drop off a cliff from this perspective, approach with caution and you'll soon see a series of steep, wide-set steps in the hillside leading down toward the tidepools. Partway down the steps, pause a moment to admire the fascinating sandstone cliffs to the south of you, sculpted by rivulets of rain.

Once you reach the bottom of the steps, continue south along the rocky shelves of sedimentary rock, which date back some 76 million years to the Cretaceous Period and have been tilted and lifted to the surface through seismic faulting. Look closely and you may see fossilized ammonite and other shells embedded in this rock.

Top: Watch for sleeping harbor seals resting along the water's edge.
Bottom: Anemones and hermit crabs viewed in a "Middle Zone" tidepool.

As you continue southward, there is no official route so explore the mini pools and niches of the "High" and "Middle Zones" as the tide safely allows. Always use your own best judgment when exploring coastal shore and keep your kids close to you—sneaker waves happen. Watch for assorted anemone, black tegula snails, Kellet's whelk, and giant keyhole limpets in this zone.

During the lowest tides, you'll be able to scramble down another level or two to pools and coves thick with purple and green seaweed. Some of the creatures you may encounter in the "Low Zone" include knobby and bat stars, purple urchin, nudibranchs, and the two-spotted octopus.

As you near the southernmost point of this trail (and main parking/access point), you may find the crowd thickens greatly. But this may also be your chance to spot a knowledgeable ranger who can point you to some fascinating finds in this busy area.

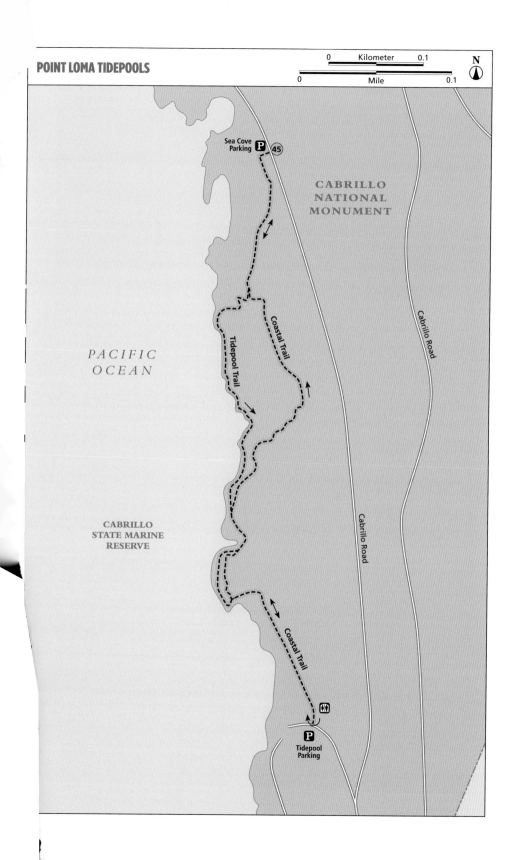

POINT LOMA TIDEPOOLS

0   Kilometer   0.1

0   Mile   0.1

N

CABRILLO
NATIONAL
MONUMENT

Sea Cove
Parking   P   45

Coastal Trail

Tidepool Trail

PACIFIC
OCEAN

Cabrillo Road

Cabrillo Road

CABRILLO
STATE MARINE
RESERVE

Coastal Trail

P
Tidepool
Parking

Venturing out to the "Low Zone" during a negative tide at Point Loma tidepools.

When ready, about-face and watch for the impressive, steep, wooden steps leading up and up from the tidepools to the Coastal Trail. Continue north along the trail past occasional sagebrush, keeping an eye out for any of the 346 species of birds that can be seen on Point Loma—a prime stop along the Pacific Flyway (see the Cabrillo Birding Guide at www.nps.gov/cabr/learn/bird-guide.htm for more).

Winter hikers should also keep an eye out toward the Pacific from along the Coastal Trail, as it's prime whale-watching season for Pacific gray whales traveling to and from the warmer waters of Baja California.

The hike concludes back at the trailhead and parking area where you began.

MILES AND DIRECTIONS

0.0   Start at the trailhead.

0.1   Take the right fork toward the ocean (southwest).

0.2   At the bottom of the steps, proceed south along the informal trail.

0.5   Arrive at the southern tidepool access point (busiest); turn back when ready.

0.6   Take the signed stairs up to Coastal Trail; continue north.

1.0   Return to the trailhead.

POINT LOMA'S FIRST PEOPLE

Though the Cabrillo National Monument may be named for a Spanish explorer who arrived in 1542, human activity on Point Loma dates back at least 9,000 years. Those earliest known inhabitants of the region are the people of the Kumeyaay Nation, whose cultural heritage and dialects persevere today among thirteen federally recognized tribes in the United States and four bands in Northern Baja California, Mexico. If you're planning a visit to nearby Balboa Park, you can learn more about the Kumeyaay People at the Museum of Us, which includes a special exhibit on Kumeyaay astronomy: the Kumeyaay Cosmology Dome.